Arguments for Socialism

Series editor: John Harrison

'As we plunge deeper into the crisis caused by monetarism and militarism, more and more people will be turning to socialist ideas to find out more about socialism and what socialists are saying.

Arguments for Socialism is developing as an essential reading list for the interested as well as the committed and offers a compact library of essential background information and clear analysis.' *Tony Benn*

Other Arguments for Socialism

Take Over the City: The Case for Public Ownership
of Financial Institutions
Richard Minns

Getting It Together: Women as Trade Unionists
Jenny Beale

More Than We Can Chew: The Crazy World of Food and Farming
Charlie Clutterbuck and Tim Lang

It Makes You Sick: The Politics of the NHS
Colin Thunhurst

Hard Times: The World Economy in Turmoil
Bob Sutcliffe

The Cuts Machine: The Politics of Public Expenditure
David Hall

Due South: Socialists and World Development
Jeremy Hill and Hilary Scannell

Planning is Good for You: The Case for Popular Control
George Blazyca

Blowing the Whistle: The Politics of Sport
Garry Whannel

Making It Public: Evidence and Action against Privatisation
Dexter Whitfield

Hidden Hands: Women and Economic Policies
Anne Phillips

Thatcher and Friends: The Anatomy of the Tory Party
John Ross

The British in Ireland
A Suitable Case for Withdrawal

Geoffrey Bell

Pluto Press

First published in 1984 by Pluto Press Limited,
The Works, 105a Torriano Avenue,
London NW5 2RX
and Pluto Press Australia Limited,
PO Box 199, Leichhardt, New South Wales 2040, Australia

Copyright © Geoffrey Bell, 1984

British Library Cataloguing in Publication Data
Bell, Geoffrey. 1947
The British in Ireland.—(Arguments for socialism)
1. Northern Ireland—Politics and government
   I. Title   II. Series
   941.6082   DA990.U4
   ISBN 0-86104-510-6

Cover designed by Clive Challis A Gr R
Computerset by Promenade Graphics Limited
Block 23a Lansdown Industrial Estate, Cheltenham GL51 8PL
Printed and bound in Great Britain
by Richard Clay (The Chaucer Press) Limited, Bungay, Suffolk

Contents

1. The Other Irish Problem / 1
The problem of the British left / 2
The Two Nations theory / 7
Why can't they be more like the English? / 9
The debate in the Labour Party / 11

2. Why Ireland? / 14
A version of history / 14
What has it got to do with us? / 16
No Irish allowed / 18
English reform/Irish revolution / 25

3. Why Northern Ireland? / 29
The revolt of 'England's best' / 33
Partition / 36
The Anglo-Irish Treaty / 39
The 'carnival of reaction' / 40

4. The Republicans / 43
The violent past / 44
The violent present / 46
Nationalism and socialism / 48
Socialists and nationalism / 51
The Provisionals / 54

5. The Loyalists / 60
Paisleyism / 60
Ordinary workers? / 62

The socialist explanation / 65
The labour aristocracy / 67
The Protestant culture / 69
Loyal to what? / 72

6. The Unions / 75
The history / 76
The civil rights intervention / 79
The challenge of sectarianism / 81
The challenge unanswered / 84
Leaders and strikers / 86

7. Why Britain? / 89
The public's opinion / 90
A consensus of opinion? / 91
An honest broker? / 93
Old generals / 95
New generals / 97
Irish threats and promises / 98

8. Why Socialism? / 102
The oldest colony / 103
The oldest settlers / 104
The blood-bath theory / 107
The cause of labour / 110
The cause of Ireland / 114

A Guide to Reading / 116

1.
The Other Irish Problem

In May 1969 *New Left Review*, the doyen of the British intellectual left, published an article on Northern Ireland. It was a discussion between members of People's Democracy, a group on the radical wing of the civil rights movement who had been demanding social, economic and political rights for Catholics – and getting clubbed by the police for their trouble. In the next decade this particular edition of Britain's foremost marxist journal became something of a collector's item, since it was the only one to address itself to the question of Ireland.

In the autumn of 1969, few would have predicted such a silence. It was the era of May 1968, the Prague Spring, the mass protests against US policy in Vietnam; west and east, capitalist hegemony and Stalinist orthodoxy were being equally challenged.

The cause of Ireland seemed tailor-made for these times of protest and solidarity. There on the doorstep of the British left stood the six counties of Northern Ireland, a slum whose absentee Westminster landlord had allowed the decay to set in to such an extent that the only solution seemed to lie in a fleet of political bulldozers.

One-third of the citizens of this state were discriminated against in voting rights, housing and jobs because of their Catholic religion. One political party, the Unionists, had enjoyed uninterrupted power since 1921. The Unionist leadership was redolent of English high Toryism of a bygone age: it was composed of gentry, landlords and ex-British Army officers who clung to their old and often lowly rank long after their uniforms were in mothballs. Those who followed the leaders seemed similarly anachronistic. Every 12 July 100,000 of them marched in their bowler hats and orange sashes, brandishing swords and pikes and banners emblazoned with portraits of defunct British monarchs.

The pomp and finery of these 'Orangemen' disguised a threadbare economy in which unemployment rarely fell below 10 per cent, and a legal system which allowed the flogging and imprisonment without trial of political dissidents.

For all this Britain was ultimately responsible, since, on the Statute Book at least, Westminster still had the power to overrule the Northern Irish parliament. This power was rarely used, and in the decades up to the 1960s, and even with the advent of the 1964 Labour government, the Northern Ireland slum was left to fester. While Harold Wilson promised modernisation, and hailed the transforming power of 'the white heat of technology', the Northern Irish parliament's only concession to the new age was to extend political censorship to gramophone records.

There was so much to kick against in the Northern Ireland of the 1960s, that British liberals, radicals and socialists might have been expected to add their voices to the protest. Even more so as the years went by, and social and economic conditions deteriorated still further. More oppressive laws were passed, unarmed demonstrators were shot, opponents of Unionism jailed without trial: by the beginning of the 1980s 2,000 had died from political violence. With 1981 came the obscenity of the H Block deaths, as the hunger strikers of Long Kesh, refused better conditions and political status, starved themselves to the grave. Among them was Bobby Sands, elected to serve as an Honourable Member in the House of Commons.

The problem of the British left

In London the demonstration at the death of Bobby Sands drew a mere 3,000 people, a number which indicated that apathy towards Ireland still far outweighed popular indig-

The Other Irish Problem

nation. Throughout the 1970s the picture had been the same: by and large, the class of 1968 did not care to wave their banners about Northern Ireland. Which brings us to another Irish problem – the problem of the British left.

This problem has various aspects, but all of them begin with the question: What to do about Ireland? Before the 1969 troubles, the Communist Party's answer was unequivocal. The 1968 revised edition of *The British Road to Socialism* declared that 'the enforced partition of Ireland should be ended and British troops withdrawn from Northern Ireland, leaving the Irish free to realise their united republic.'

This had been the traditional view of the British marxist left since the Anglo–Irish Treaty enforced partition in 1921, but it was not common currency with all those who called themselves socialists. Both the Labour Party and its left wing, the Independent Labour Party (ILP), had welcomed the 1921 Treaty, and in 1949 the Labour government's Ireland Act further strengthened partition by giving the Unionist-dominated parliament the right to veto any moves towards a united Ireland. Throughout this period there were lobby groups within the Labour Party which opposed its policies – the Friends of Ireland, in the late 1940s and early 1950s, was one – but the general mood both at leadership level and in the rank and file was one of indifference. This laissez-faire approach to Ireland dragged on throughout the 1970s, and the Labour Party's answer to the question of what to do about Ireland continued to be: As little as we can get away with.

The field was left open for others whose answers were similar to the 1968 Communist Party line. The Troops Out Movement (TOM) was founded in the early 1970s around the demand for troop withdrawal and self-determination for the Irish people as a whole; although it was the largest group campaigning around the Irish issue in Britain, its active membership never reached four figures. The Labour Party's lack of interest remained a better measure of British working-class attitudes than the TOM's militancy.

As for the Communist Party, once British troops adopted an active rather than a passive role in Northern Ireland, it changed its line. An article in the July 1973 issue of *Marxism Today* described urgent consultations with the Irish Communist Party after the 1969 troubles, and spoke of the need for a revised policy which,

> without in any way abandoning our basic principles in support of the Irish people's right to reunite their country, would meet the demands of the immediate situation, make possible an advance for the democratic movement in Northern Ireland, and so open the way to new possibilities for a solution to Ireland's basic long-term problem — full unity and full independence.

The article concluded that the hub of the present struggle in Northern Ireland was for democratic rights and against repression and discrimination. Victories in this would pave the way towards uniting the working class of Northern Ireland, and create new conditions for achieving a political solution to the partition of Ireland. British domination could then be ended and the Irish people given the opportunity of reuniting their country. The article took pains to stress that the Irish struggle must be the concern of the British working class, since British imperialism was the main factor sustaining continuing repression in Northern Ireland.

The strategic thinking displayed here is important, for it points up the major issues which affected the British left's capacity to relate to Ireland in the 1970s. Those were: the disunity of the Northern Irish working class; the problem of how a united Ireland could be achieved; the role of British imperialism, and the role of the British working class in the struggle. Another aspect of the left's dilemma — the thorny question of Republican resistance — did not, of course, arise in those 1969 Communist Party discussions, for the main expression of that resistance, the Provisional IRA, did not yet exist. At that stage there was still some credibility in the CP view — similar to that of People's Democracy — that the main issue in Northern Ireland was civil rights.

The collapse of the civil rights movement and the rise of the Provisionals in 1971–2 brought a new and grimmer reality. August 1971 saw British troops being used to enforce the Unionist government's internment policy; January 1972 brought the Bloody Sunday shootings in Derry, and March of that year saw Westminster's assumption of direct responsibility for Northern Ireland.

For some these events were ample evidence that attempts to reform the Northern Ireland state were useless. Two days after internment the Provisional IRA put it this way:

> The war declared on the Irish people by the British Army in the occupied area of our country has reached a critical stage . . . the Army Council of the Irish Republican Army strongly appeals to the Irish race, at home and abroad, to give every assistance to the . . . gallant resistance to aggression of a foreign power.
>
> The root cause of foreign aggression is historically rooted in the unnatural division of our country and its domination by British imperialism. It has taken fifty years of corrupt, rotten government. North and South, to expose the futility and injustice of the 1921 partition settlement . . . Much has been endured at the hands of the British forces, but irrespective of the cost, the Irish people will not flinch from any suffering, shirk any responsibility or weaken in their determination to achieve the status of a free and independent Nation.

There was a directness in this analysis which was absent from the strategic hedging and self-revisions of the Communist Party document. But was it really so simple? A case of war on the Irish people by the British Army? Aggression by a foreign power? And would peace really break out as soon as Ireland became a free and independent nation? For the British left, it was all rather hard to swallow, let alone rally the working class around. And so, once again, the masses did not take to the streets over Ireland.

The sceptics had a number of objections. First, since the surplus value produced by the Belfast and Derry workers was less than adequate to satisfy the City shareholders, the relationship between the British ruling class and Ireland could hardly be seen as a classical imperialist one. Second, most people in Northern Ireland, including a majority of the working class, seemed to be crying out for Britain to stay. Third, the combatants in Northern Ireland appeared to be defined by religion rather than nationality or class. And, finally, while recognising that British soldiers did brutal things, many feared even bloodier occurrences if the troops left prematurely.

In the mid-1970s Tom Nairn, one of the more thoughtful left critics of the Republican line, argued that there was no anti-imperialist struggle in Ireland in the usual sense, nor was there a chance of that struggle moving from a nationalist to a socialist or class-based one. Nairn predicted that if the 'troops out' advocates had their way, there would follow a civil war and the establishment of two utterly reactionary states in which:

> Every single representative of the Communist Parties, the Trotskyists . . . and the other sets of communist initials who have assumed 'correct revolutionary positions' on Ireland would be in prison or dead. Consistent to the end, the few survivors in London would blame the catastrophe on imperialist plotters and lackeys. Labour Party politics on both sides of the frontier would dwindle to even greater insignificance than today. Glumly pleased that its diagnosis had proved so right – 'The Irish are all mad' – the British public would forget about the problem for good.

The trouble with such theoretical KOs is that an alternative has to be pushed into the ring. Many contenders were weighed in. For Nairn the 'answer' was an independent Ulster, free of Britain and the rest of Ireland. For the Communist Party, as already mentioned, it was the 'revolution by stages' theory: first, secure democratic rights, then unite Northern Ireland's working class, then work towards national unity, and, finally, achieve socialism. Other solutions included a phased British withdrawal; replacing the army with a United Nations force; setting up 'workers' defence units' in which both Protestants and Catholics would serve; redrawing the border; creating a federal Ireland with or without links to the British state – and many others, each more schematic than the last. But perhaps the most daring departure of all was the Two Nations theory, which called for socialists to ditch the entire cause of antipartitionism, and stand shoulder to shoulder with the Protestant workers.

The Two Nations theory

This demand originated from a group called the Irish Communist Organisation, which, to mark its infatuation with the link with Britain, changed its name to the British and Irish Communist Organisation, and worked in Ireland in front organisations like the Workers' Association and Socialists Against Nationalism. Before its conversion to Unionism, the (B)ICO's claim to a footnote in the annals of Irish socialism was its break with the Irish Communist Party in order to safeguard Stalinist orthodoxy in the face of Khrushchev's criticisms.

Numerically small though the (B)ICO was in the early 1970s, its Two Nations theory was to enjoy a growing popularity in left-wing circles both in Ireland and Britain. Among those who supported it – not always unreservedly – were the leadership of the Irish Labour Party, particularly its main ideologue, Conor Cruise O'Brien; the Northern Irish Labour Party, and the research department of the British Labour Party. Aspects of the theory were also adopted by the Althusserian school of marxists, the Official Republican movement, *Militant* groups within the British and Irish Labour Parties, and the Eurocommunist wing of the Communist Party.

It would be wrong to say either that there was one definitive theory, or that the influence of the various branches of it should be held responsible for the failure of the Irish cause to take root in the British socialist movement. What can be suggested, however, is that parts of the theory dovetailed rather neatly with long-standing British prejudices, and, in that respect, became a convenient argument for keeping the struggle for Irish unity at arm's length.

In the words of various advocates of the Two Nations theory, the argument ran something like the following.

The Protestants and Catholics in Ireland constituted two distinct national groups. By the end of the nineteenth century, argued the (B)ICO, the Protestant working class were opposed to Irish Home Rule because they saw Irish nationalism as 'a movement of farmers and gombeen men who were hostile to trade unionism and to everything they regarded as progressive.' The partition of Ireland recognised the two nations, Tom Nairn argued, and therefore 'the democratic, that is to say the national stage of the Irish revolution seems probably to have been as complete as it ever could be by 1921.' This led him to conclude that 'there is nothing inherently reactionary about the Protestant working class . . . or, for that matter, a natural frontier which puts Protestants in a numerical majority.' And the Labour Party pressure group, Campaign for Labour Representation, insisted that 'any move to overcome the sectional/national division in the working class of Northern Ireland . . . must therefore be made within the framework of the UK.'

Armed with an analysis which defended partition and the Unionists' right to stay within the UK, the Two-Nationists' evaluation of the combatants in post-1968 Ireland was very different from the traditionalists' view. In 1972, writing in the influential *Socialist Register*, A.Boserup maintained, 'In the nationalist struggle now going on – but not, of course, in a genuine socialist struggle if there had been one – the British authorities may be assumed to be indifferent.' As for the Protestant working class, he continued, 'its advanced character is perhaps most evident in the remarkable restraint and discipline it showed when . . . it was exposed to the provocation of the IRA.' And when Protestant groups did take the field against Republicans, another Two Nationist, Dick Barry of the research department of the Labour Party, dubbed them 'counter-terrorist organisations'.

The individuals and organisations quoted above would not necessarily agree with each other on every single point. Where a consensus can be detected, however, is in an impatience with the whole 'national question'. A wish – at times, a demand – that it would disappear and allow the bread-and-butter issues of socialist agitation to flourish. For the Two-Nationists, working-class unity was the prerequisite for social and political advancement; its attainment, therefore, was an absolute priority. The national question, as everyone knew, only divided the working classes of Northern Ireland. Notions of Irish unity, then, were either illegitimate – as the Two-Nations theory insisted – or 'long-term goals' – the 1969 Communist Party line.

This sort of thinking begged certain questions. For instance, how was this workers' unity to be achieved? How was partition to be driven from the minds of Northern Irish workers? They were important issues, not least because when those left theorists asserted the right of 'Protestant Ulster' to stay British, and decried the campaign of the Republicans, they were uncomfortably close to the public stances of the British ruling class. Indeed, in first elaborating their theory, the (B)ICO had used the testimonies of an early-twentieth-century Tory, W.F.Moneypenny, the *Times* editorials of 1912, and the Tory leader Bonar Law who stated: 'There are two peoples in Ireland separated from each other by a gulf of religion, or race, and above all of prejudice, far deeper than that which separates Ireland as a whole from the rest of the UK.'

So, if the pro-partitionists of the left and the Tories had such similar views of Irish national reality, how in practice was a differentiation to be made?

Why can't they be more like the English?

One suggestion came from the Labour Party's research department, and a small pressure group within the party called the Campaign for Labour Representation (in Ireland). According to them, if the Labour Party organised and stood for election in Northern Ireland, the traditional Unionist and nationalist attachments of the working class would break down. The same argument was made by the Militant Tendency in the Labour Party when it called for the formation of a Northern Ireland Labour Party. Even those on the far left who usually stressed the national question and placed Irish socialist politics in an all-Ireland context could be found blaming the 'subjective' factor for the apparent lack of socialist progress within Northern Ireland. In the spring of 1982 the Socialist Workers' Party complained: 'The tragedy is that there has not been built in Northern Ireland a genuinely socialist organisation prepared to relate to . . . class experience.' This may have been true, but such verdicts once again begged the question. Why had no 'socialist organisation' been built? In the early 1970s the SWP had itself tried to establish a 'sister' organisation in Ireland, the Socialist Workers' Movement, but like many similar organisations, this had failed to attract more than a faithful few.

Other prescriptions – usually concocted by political doctors in Britain – were also tested on Northern Ireland's working class, with high hopes that the patient would soon be cured of its obsession with nationalities. In March 1977 the executive committee of the Communist Party reported the 'encouraging popular movements against sectarianism and violence' of the Better Life for All Campaign which had been mounted by the Northern Ireland Committee of the Irish Congress of Trade Unions:

> The campaign also makes demands on other issues such as full employment, decent housing, equal educational opportunities and adequate social services. It therefore helps build the broad democratic movement and unites the working people around *class* demands. It has been able to establish support on both sides of the sectarian divide and has now over 300,000 signatures for its declaration.

Official backing, the report stressed, had been given by the British, Welsh and Scottish TUCs as well as the European Federation of Trade Unions.

Equally triumphalist was the *Militant* when its panacea, the establishment of a trade-union-backed Labour Party, got under way. In March 1981 the newspaper reported:

> History was made in the City of Derry when the Derry Trades Council decided to stand candidates in the forthcoming local government elections. This momentous decision is of importance not only to the working class of Derry but for workers throughout Northern Ireland and indeed within these islands.

These optimistic declarations, like the numerous Westminster proposals for a Northern Ireland settlement made throughout the 1970s, bore little fruit. The Better Life for All Campaign was dead before the end of the decade. And in the May 1981 local government elections the Derry Trades Council candidates received votes of 75, 88, and 164.

The elections themselves were a forceful reminder of Irish reality. The Protestant working class swung even further towards Paisleyism, whose sectarian 'No Surrender' politics had, over the previous ten years, been stealing popular loyalist support from the Official Unionists. For the Catholic community the period of the elections was dominated by the starving hunger strikers, and voting was by pure instinct. In the Westminster by-election Bobby Sands was voted in for Fermanagh and South Tyrone, while in the local government elections other candidates who supported the strikers were returned. The hunger strike made its mark also in the general elections held in Southern Ireland around the same time, where two candidates who supported the strike were elected. Workers' unity, it seemed, was just a mirage, Or, as the Labour Party national executive told the party conference in 1981: 'Labour politics in Northern Ireland are in a tragic and polarised position. No working-class organisation exists which is capable of bringing Catholics and Protestants together inside a single political organisation to further their interests as workers.'

The debate in the Labour Party

The 1981 NEC statement was the first detailed declaration of policy on Ireland which the party had made for 60 years. This fact was as significant as the actual content of the statement, for it suggested that Northern Ireland had at last come in from the outer limits of British socialism and penetrated the consciousness of the Labour Party itself. Confirmation of this came later in the conference when the Constituency Labour Parties submitted over 50 resolutions and amendments on Ireland – almost the highest number on any issue that year, and more than had been submitted in the whole 60-year stretch since partition.

The NEC statement had been under preparation for two years, whereas the resolutions had a more immediate inspiration in the public outcry over the hunger strikes. But integral to the thinking of both was the election of Bobby Sands and the massive Catholic support for the hunger strikers. Suddenly it was no longer viable to file the Irish situation away under the old clichéd labels of 'terrorism', 'sectarianism' and 'criminal elements'. And although the Labour left and their supporters in the Constituency Labour Parties by and large held back from endorsing the specific aims of the hunger strikers, their resolutions did express support for the Republican goal – British withdrawal and a united Ireland. Among the active rank and file, anti-partition won an easy victory. The withdrawal resolution won overwhelming support from the Constituency Labour Party section of the 1981 conference; the trade union block vote, however, ensured its defeat.

Instead, victory went to the hesitant and self-contradictory NEC statement, which endorsed the 'long-term' aim of Irish unity but stressed also that, 'the people of Northern Ireland will not be expelled from the United Kingdom against their wishes.' This was not to mean, however, 'a veto on political development in the hands of the Unionist leaders'. On the one hand, the document stated that the consent of the people of Northern Ireland was to be obtained before any constitutional changes were made. On the other, a proposal for a referendum was voted out by the NEC prior to publication.

On some issues the statement took positions similar to the *Militant* and the Communist Party. Although unity was the 'long-term' aim, the 'prerequisite' was 'the creation of greater unity between and within the working class in Northern Ireland'. The establishment of a Northern Ireland Labour Party 'rooted in the trade unions' was promoted, 'to give a clear political lead on the social and economic issues which unite Catholic and Protestant workers'.

Whatever the merits of these arguments, or the counter

ones put forward by the traditionalists, who insisted on Irish unity as the precondition for progress and working-class advancement, at least the pieces of the Irish jigsaw had now been shuffled by the major British working-class party. The leadership had at last acknowledged Ireland as a suitable debate for socialists. Over the next couple of years the actions of some party members – such as GLC leader Ken Livingstone, who publicly pledged support for British withdrawal – made sure that it remained so. Events in Ireland – the electoral victories of Sinn Fein for instance – insisted that it had to be so.

The rest of this book will look at the constituent parts of this debate. These include the historical origins of Northern Ireland, Republicanism and loyalism, the capacity of trade unionism to heal divisions in the Northern Irish working class, the possibility of British withdrawal, and, finally, what might follow such a withdrawal.

To introduce this examination of Northern Ireland's relevance for socialists, a brief outline of the British radical tradition as regards Ireland follows.

2.
Why Ireland?

On 3 March 1917, the *New Statesman* observed: 'The Irishman regards himself as the heir of Irish history: the Englishman is inclined to behave as though there was no such thing as Irish history.'

The jibe is as relevant now as it was then. During the current Irish crisis, how often have the British been heard to complain that the Irish 'dwell on the past', and that they should instead forgive, forget, look to the future? It's only common sense, they think. The Irish troublemakers who are meant to take these exhortations to heart hear only a convicted prisoner pleading from the dock. 'Irish history', the *New Statesman* went on, 'exists as a witness in the Irishman's favour. It is the history of the decadence of a nation – owing to the absence of freedom.' For this reason, then, no proper insight into Ireland in the 1980s can be gained without an appreciation of what went before.

A version of history

A summary of Ireland's history was written by a pamphleteer called the 'Man of Kent' in 1834. It outlined how in the twelfth century Henry II used 'English mercenaries' to 'seize the lands of the Irish' and how later 'an English army defeated the Irish and laid their country waste with fire and sword, sparing neither age nor sex.' The Man of Kent went on to quote the 'Infamous Statute of Kilkenny' of 1270, which contained the decree: 'If an Englishman kill an Irishman he shall pay a fine of Sixpence.' In 1461, the pamphlet records: 'The English passed several laws and set a price on every native Irishman.' Then, in 1630, 'The Irish are conquered by Cromwell, who decrees their entire extirpation and finally gives them the province of Connaught for shelter; in their flight thither many hundreds are shot and otherwise butchered by the wantonness of the soldiers.' The history ends in 1800, when 'the union with England effected by the corruption of the Anglo-Irish Parliament . . . is resisted by the people, who are treated as rebels, many are hanged and transported, and others dealt with by martial law, to the disgrace of humanity.'

The Man of Kent's conclusion leaves no doubt as to his sympathies:

> The anti-Christian, sordid and selfish policy of England has dealt in a chain of unbroken oppression for the last 700 years; thereby impairing her own resources and reducing the inhabitants of one of the most fertile and prolific spots of the globe, to the lowest state of misery and crime, which was ever the lot of man to bear.

This version of history may be faulted for detail, but its general thrust is not inaccurate. Yet the Man of Kent was only one of many English radicals – today they might even be called extremists – who over the last centuries have railed against the maltreatment of the Irish. In 1833 the radical republican Richard Carlile argued in his newspaper *Gauntlet*: 'Justice for Ireland is the first principle of an Englishman's present political honesty.' This moral stance had been taken up before, and has been echoed since, for, given the barbarisms which the Irish have suffered at the hands of their conquerors, it has never been hard to sympathise with their plight.

A few facts can be added to flesh out the Man of Kent's account. In 1535 Henry VIII's agents slaughtered a rebellious garrison at Maynooth – after the garrison had surrendered. In 1649 Cromwell massacred the townspeople of Wexford – 3,000 men, women and children. In the year of 1740–1 as many as 400,000 Irish died in a famine exacerbated by the dreadful social and economic conditions of the previous 100 years. In 1798, floggings, mutilations, torture and death were meted out to 15,000 people in the aftermath of the United Irishmen Rising. And most catastrophic of all, the famine years of 1845–51, when one million died of starvation and the typhus and cholera which followed.

Not surprisingly, the Irish did not simply turn the other cheek. They protested, peacefully or otherwise, only to find that their protests brought upon their heads a system of law and order whose repressive ingenuity knew no bounds. On different occasions, chieftains were bribed, exiled or executed, a price was put on the head of every priest, Catholic Irish were barred from public office, the Irish language was proscribed, and coercive law after coercive law sent rebellious souls to meet their maker. Most pernicious of all, perhaps, was the confiscation of land held by the natives – in 1641 Catholics owned 59 per cent of the land of Ireland; by 1703 the figure had dropped to 14 per cent.

Acknowledging this catalogue of horrors the London *Cap of Liberty* commented in 1819: 'Alas poor Ireland, how hast thou been abused and degraded'. Others, too, spoke out against the subjection of the Irish. In 1794 the London Corresponding Society, the first political organisation in Britain whose membership was largely proletarian, protested: 'If we look to Ireland we find that the acknowledged privilege of the people to meet for the support and protection of their rights and liberties, is attempted by terror to be taken away.' And 50 years later the leading English Chartist William Lovett wrote in *Howett's Journal*: 'The primary cause of most of the evils which afflict Ireland . . . can be traced to the legislative and executive powers . . . vested in the few instead of the many, those few having legislated for and governed Ireland for their own individual interests and aggrandisement.'

What has it got to do with us?

While it is important to know that English progressives were condemning the situation in Ireland, what their humanitarian statements failed to do was to offer an analysis which could convince those influenced by the traditions of English radicalism that Ireland was integral to their struggle.

An early attempt at a more analytical approach was attempted by the Levellers in the seventeenth century. Protesting at the despatch of soldiers to Ireland in the 1640s, the Levellers couched their argument in terms of the troops' self-interest:

> As things now stand, to what end should you hazard your lives against the Irish: have you not been fighting in England for rights and liberties that you are yet deluded of? And that too, when none can hinder you of them, but your own officers under whom you have fought? And will you go on still to kill, slay and murder men, to make [the officers] as absolute lords and masters over Ireland as you have made them over England . . . Or if you intend not this, or would be sorry to see no better effects of your undertakings, it certainly concerns you in the first place, and before you go, to see these evils reformed here.

In not so many words, the Levellers were saying that the enemy was a class enemy, and the struggle began at home. But it was to little or no avail, for, in the end, regiments otherwise sympathetic to the radicalism of the Levellers did join Cromwell in his Irish slaughter, and what mutinies there were in the army of the Parliamentarians were caused by wage disputes. During the suppression of the United Irishmen rebellion, 150 years later, the London Corresponding Society made a similar appeal to soldiers, warning that any threat to Irish civil liberties was also a threat to the English common people:

> When a people once permits government to violate the genuine principles of liberty, encroachment will be grafted on encroachment, evil will grow upon evil, violation will follow violation and power will engender power, till the liberties of *ALL* will be held at despotic command.

As details of the methods used to put down the Rising slowly filtered back to Britain, other English radicals warned that the same treatment might be in store for them.

In 1817 William Sherwin's weekly *Political Register* asked: 'The tortures in Ireland – is it probable the same system is intended for this country?' And 16 years later, Richard Carlile's *Gauntlet* was again sounding the alarm about the import–export cycle of repression:

> These Whigs with Lord Grey at their head have brought a Bill into the House of Lords to put all life and property in Ireland at their disposal, to arm themselves with despotic power such as is only known in Africa . . . If this be allowed to pass as to Ireland, it will soon be tried in England; and I am for making a stand against it now.

No Irish allowed

Carlile went on to 'damn those who cry patience while a sword is being sharpened for the throats of the long-oppressed people of Ireland,' but the problem he faced, just like the Levellers and the London Corresponding Society, was not only those who cried patience, but also those who showed indifference or hostility to his cause.

The English proletariat, for instance, was busy waging its own anti-Irish battles on home ground. Throughout the eighteenth and nineteenth centuries there were clashes between British and Irish labourers. The reasons for these outbreaks were various.

In 1736, when mobs of up to 5,000 attacked the homes and public houses of Irish immigrants in east London, the combatants were no ruffians or lumpen proletariat. Rather, they were respectable wage-earners, the backbone of London's working class, infuriated by the sacking of English workers and the employment of Irish ones at a half or two-thirds of their wages.

In 1858 a riot flared in Hyde Park when Irish immigrants opposed a meeting in support of the Italian republican and anti-papalist Garibaldi. On the other hand, in 1837 Irish in Preston were mobbed when they marched in support of a radical and pro-Irish candidate. Other clashes – for instance, those in Liverpool in 1819 and 1835, and in Birmingham in

1868 – had a religious basis. On more than one occasion – notably in the Penrith riots of 1846 – the prime factor was British xenophobia.

Writing to his brother about the east London riots of 1736, Sir Robert Walpole commented: 'Their cry and complaint was of being underworked and starved by the Irish.' This cry and complaint went on into the next century, so that in 1845 Friedrich Engels was noting in *The Conditions of the English Working Class*: 'The wages of English working men are forced down further and further in every branch in which the Irish compete with them.'

It is clear that at times cheap Irish labour did threaten the employment and conditions of some English workers. As a Manchester factory-owner testified in 1835: 'The moment I have a turn-out [strike] and am fast for hands I send to Ireland for ten, fifteen, or twenty families.'

Yet on other occasions it was Irish immigrants who took the lead in working-class militancy. In 1836, an employer giving evidence before a parliamentary commission complained: 'Where there is discontent, or a disposition to combine, or turn-outs among the work people, the Irish are the leaders; they are the most difficult to reason with and convince on subjects of wages and regulations in factories.'

It was not only the issue of economic competition, then, which prevented the English proletariat identifying with the Irish. Nor can it simply be laid at the feet of the national chauvinism entrenched in so many English commoners. There was also the question of the yawning gap between their cultural, economic and political traditions.

Religion was certainly an issue here, as evidenced by London's Gordon Riots of 1780, when the cry of 'No Popery' was on everyone's lips. For the English radical, Catholicism was associated with superstition, royal despotism, political and social conservatism, and a general 'backwardness' in its adherents.

Setting off for Ireland, Cromwell, the scourge of the British monarchy, pledged: 'We come by the assistance of God to hold forth and maintain the lustre and glory of English liberty.' Such self-righteous bombast, usually accompanied by eulogies citing the progressiveness of English or Scottish Protestantism, struck a sympathetic chord in many English radicals. In 1835 we find Richard Cobden, one of the most famous of all, writing:

> During all that period in time which has sufficed to enable the other states in Europe to emerge from barbarism . . . Ireland has never enjoyed one age of perfect security or peace. She has consequently, unlike any other nation, no era of literature, commerce or arts to boast of . . .
>
> Poets have feigned a golden age for this, as for every other country : but it never existed . . .
>
> But there exists, apart from all intolerant or party feelings on the question a cause, and we believe a primary one, of the retrograde position as compared with England and Scotland, in the circumstances of the Roman Catholic religion being the faith of the people.

Cobden's attitudes to Irish history are remarkable. Had he forgotten, perhaps, that during the Dark Ages of the seventh and eighth centuries, while invasions ravaged the rest of the continent, Ireland was an outpost of Christianity and literacy, and that it was Irish monks who taught the English to read and write? Did he know nothing about the wealth of Celtic literature which stemmed from those times?

But Cobden's brand of radical reformism did not have a monopoly on ignorance and prejudice. In 1845 Engels could boast an anti-Irish bias as stubborn as that of many to the right of him. In *The Conditions of the English Working Class* he wrote:

> Those Irishmen who migrate for fourpence to England, on the deck of a steamship on which they are often packed like cattle, insinuate themselves everywhere. The worst dwellings are good enough for them; their clothing causes them little trouble, so long as it holds together by a single thread; shoes they know not; their food consists of potatoes and potatoes only; whatever they earn beyond these needs they spend upon drink. What does such a race want with high wages . . . ? Drink is the only thing which makes the Irishman's life

worth having, drink and his cheery carefree
temperament; so he revels in drink to the point of the
most bestial drunkenness. The southern facile
character of the Irishman, his crudity, which places him
but little above the savage, his contempt for all human
enjoyments, in which his very crudeness make him
incapable of sharing, his filth and poverty, all favour
drunkenness. The temptation is great, he cannot resist
it, and so when he has money he gets rid of it down his
throat.

Engels was later to make up for this racism, when he fell in love with the Irish individually and collectively, and became a stalwart champion of the Irish national cause. But the fact that he could write such gibberish just a couple of years before he and Marx composed the Communist Manifesto was a measure of how deeply anti-Irish feeling was ingrained in British society, even the left wing of it.

Inevitably, such opinions had an impact on Ireland. 'There are no enemies of Ireland more bitter, more contemptuous, more immitigable than the Radicals of England,' said the Dublin *Freeman's Journal* in March 1843. This view was contested by Patrick O'Higgins, an Irish radical active in the English Chartist movement. 'I know the English radicals,' he wrote in the columns of the Chartist newspaper *Northern Star*, 'I know their hatred of oppression; I know their love of liberty, and their anxious desire to see justice, ample justice, done to Ireland.'

The editor of the *Northern Star*, Fergus O'Conner, was one individual who made dedicated efforts to link the cause of Irish national liberty with that of the British working class. He was well qualified for this, for as an MP in Ireland he had battled on the dominant political issues of the time – repeal of the Union and Catholic emancipation. He had broken with Daniel O'Connell, the leader of the Union Repeal movement, because of O'Connell's conservatism, and had gone to the North of England to become the leader of the Chartist movement in the late 1830s and 1840s. In the columns of the *Northern Star*, he argued the twin causes of popular democracy in England and repeal of the Union in Ireland. An editorial of May 1843 puts the case eloquently:

> Here then are avowals which leave no doubt as to the course which has been determined on. 'War, war to the knife against Repeal is the watchword of the day'; and th struggle against the rising spirit of liberty is to be shifted from the English to the Irish shore. The full phial of oppression and the full measure of iniquity are now to be served up to Ireland, and she is to be coerced 'in earnest'.
>
> What should be the conduct of the people – the English people – while the struggle pends? Should they stand tamely by and see Ireland immolated without coming to the rescue? Should they aid the tyrants and send 'fighting men' to dye her fields with blood and 'thank God 'twas our boys who did it'? Oh! No, no, no! . . . Every nail fastened in the coffin of Irish independence is a dagger piercing the heart of English liberty; a rivet making more fast our manacles . . . Wheresoever the flag of liberty contends with tyranny there do we uplift our weapon for it, no matter by whom it may be carried . . .
>
> Let us array ourselves – English and Scotch and Irishman – under one common banner, with the flag of freedom and the Charter waving over us . . . and the sacred tree of liberty shall take root as one in Britain and in Ireland, and it shall flourish under the fostering genius of democracy, until its blessed fruits, social justice and individual enjoyment, causing the flush of happiness to mantle on each face, shall pleasingly but quietly proclaim our triumph.

Romantic, perhaps, but O'Conner's argument also had teeth. He perceived that the interests of the British ruling class were identical in Ireland and Britain, and contended that to overthrow the political rule of that class it was necessary for the British and Irish to reinforce each other's struggle, to strike together against a common enemy. For O'Conner it was not just an idealistic principle that the working people of Ireland and Britain should unite and fight, it also made sense strategically.

In this O'Conner is borne out by the authoritative historian E.P.Thompson, who remarks that from the mid-eighteenth to the mid-nineteenth century 'England probably stood near to revolution only in 1831, when Irish unrest, rural disturbance and popular and middle-class excitement over the first Reform Bill combined to bring the country to the verge of civil war.'

The events cited by E.P.Thompson were not merely coincidental. Irish immigrants played a significant role in the reform movement, particularly in the left-wing National Union of the Working Classes, which in 1832 merged with the London-based Irish Anti-Union Association, and added repeal of the Union to its aims.

The 1790s – another crisis period for the ruling class – had also seen Irish–English radical alliances. In April 1794, for instance, the London Corresponding Society 'unanimously resolved' that: 'the approbation of the society be directed to the society of the United Irishmen in Dublin and to exhort them to persevere in their exertions to obtain justice for Ireland.' In their turn, Irish immigrants showed solidarity with the London Corresponding Society when its Jacobinism came under attack: in October 1797, for instance, an attempt to raze the home of Society leader Thomas Hardy was repulsed by 100 Society members, 'many of them Irish', an eye-witness recorded, 'armed with good shillelaghs.'

It was links like those which Fergus O'Conner sought to develop and reinforce. In 1839 he urged the Chartist convention to consider the best means of 'enlisting the support of the Irish people in furtherance of the People's Charter'; by 1842 he had succeeded in securing the inclusion of Union repeal in the second Chartist petition. A special newspaper to argue the case for an Irish–English radical alliance even appeared for a time in 1848, and there were joint-demonstrations in Britain of Chartists and Irish repealers, two of which, in May and June 1848, were forcibly broken up by police.

These developments prompted optimism in some quarters. Presenting the third Chartist petition to the House of Commons in 1848, Smith O'Brien, an Irish Chartist leader, was inspired to say: 'I am happy to think there is amongst the middle and humbler classes of this country a large amount of sympathy with Ireland . . . that amongst the Chartists there is scarce an individual who does not sympathise with the cause of Ireland.'

Unfortunately, this was an exaggeration, for the English–Irish alliance, such as it was, was due largely to the determined efforts of O'Conner and the other Irish immigrants in the Chartist movement. Other leading Chartists – such as William Lovett, and the Scottish movement – while generally sympathetic to the Irish cause, were firmly opposed to linking it with Chartist agitation. There had been a similar picture in the 1790s, too, for the London Corresponding Society's 'unanimous' pledge of support for the United Irishmen had not been won without substantial internal struggles.

Nevertheless, O'Conner's argument about the strategic importance of fusing the struggles of the British and Irish common people is borne out by the fact that the British ruling class, in the eighteenth and nineteenth centuries, was most under threat when there was a convergence of popular struggles in Ireland and Britain, and when British radical leaders were standing up and taking notice of Ireland's fight for independence.

This is hardly surprising. As Chapter 7 will demonstrate, the British ruling class has traditionally been fearful that Ireland might be used as a military and political base against it. Accordingly, when Irish revolutionaries and British radicals have recognised this ruling class as their common enemy and consequently have sought to link their struggles, its capacity to maintain authority has always tended to falter. Of course, such a unity of struggle is not always possible, and at times the class struggle in Britain has been at such a low ebb that Irish revolutionaries have had little to link up with. But certainly all the historical evidence suggests that when British radicals have included Ireland in their agitation, the effectiveness of their own general struggle against the ruling class has been increased.

Crude pragmatism, in fact, should have led the English radicals to the same conclusion as O'Conner. In the late eighteenth and early nineteenth centuries the English working class did not have the social power to make revolution by itself. It needed allies, and apart from the radical sections of the bourgeoisie, the Irish were one of the few available.

English reform/Irish revolution

As the nineteenth century progressed the indigenous working class grew in strength, organisation and self-sufficiency. British working-class history in the second half of the nineteenth century is the story of maturing self-organisation, particularly industrial; by contrast, the anti-constitutionalism of the Chartists, the National Union of the Working Classes and the London Corresponding Society was becoming a memorial to a different age. The British Empire expanded, increasing national pride and allowing to the working class a modicum of prosperity from its small share in the imperialist bounty. The great reforming ministries of Gladstone and Disraeli, the steady if slow extension of the franchise and the growth of the trade unions – all of these were potent arguments for reformism, be it the political reformism of the major parties or the ideology of trade unionism through which the workers asked for more but did so without challenging the existing economic order. The vast majority of the English working class also seemed content with the existing political order. It was not until the start of the twentieth century that the formation of their own political party, the Labour Party, got under way in earnest, and it was not until the end of the First World War that the Labour Party woke up to the need to organise on a mass basis within the working class.

In Ireland things were less peaceful. The Fenian Rising of 1867, the land revolts of the 1870s and 1880s, even the parliamentary bad manners of Charles Parnell's Home Rule Party showed that the consensus of polite politics did not travel well across the Irish Sea. The gap between the political thinking and methods of the two islands, was, if anything, widening. The British working class were hearing fewer exhortations about Ireland from their leaders, and fewer explanations as to why they shared a common cause – particularly after 1886, when the Liberal Party committed itself to Irish Home Rule, thus apparently diminishing the need for labour movement agitation. It may also be that some of the reasons given by radical pioneers for including Ireland in the British proletarian programme seemed to have lost force by the second half of the nineteenth century. The argument that repression perfected abroad would eventually be used to shackle the working class at home, for example, had lost its edge. The Coercion Acts passed with disdainful regularity by the British parliament were designed for Ireland and the Irish, and that is where they remained – not least because the passivity of the British working class rendered them superfluous.

This is, of course, a generalisation. British workers did have their battles with the existing order, and their grassroots politics. And there were still those who argued that Irish solidarity was crucial. Most notably, of course, was Karl Marx, who maintained that the Achilles' heel of the British ruling class was in Ireland, and that a defeat there would make their overthrow in Britain much easier. He perceived also that the prejudice of English workers against Irish immigrants harmed both groups in the face of a common capitalist enemy. Consequently, he and his followers organised demonstrations in support of the Irish, and introduced resolutions of solidarity at labour meetings. 'It is the task of the International everywhere to put the conflict between England and Ireland in the foreground, and everywhere to side openly with Ireland,' wrote Marx in 1870, and he set about doing just that.

There were others with a similar frame of mind. One was H.M.Hyndeman, founder of the Social Democratic Federation. The early SDF, and its forerunner, the Democratic Federation, saw Ireland as one of its major preoccupations. 'The English workers' . . . real allies are the Irish people,' said Hyndeman's *Justice* in February 1884, 'little as they have recognised it hitherto.' It was fair comment on the closing decades of the nineteenth century, for, the SDF aside, the most important socialist and labour parties of the late nineteenth and early twentieth centuries expressed no interest in Irish self-determination. The Fabians were generally hostile to it; the Independent Labour Party, founded in 1892, did not include it in its political programme; while the Labour Party and its forerunner, the Labour Representation Committee, founded in 1900, did not see fit to debate Ireland in conference until 1918. The trade unions were even more silent.

All of which meant that when Ireland once again came to dominate British politics – from 1912 to 1914, and from 1918 to 1921 – the British labour movement was unprepared theoretically and programmatically.

But although socialists had neglected to ask questions about Ireland in the preceding years, the answers, if half-buried, were still there, encapsulated in Marx's famous phrase: 'A nation which enslaves another can never be free.' Or, in the words of Fergus O'Conner: 'The liberty of Ireland is the liberty of England.' Despite the rhetoric, there was a clarity and vigour in these formulations, based as they were on the rationale that a defeat for the British ruling class in Ireland would weaken it at home. It was patently true that the Irish issue had proved an Achilles' heel more than once. It had split the Tories when Catholic emancipation was passed in 1829, and it had split the Liberals when Gladstone converted to Home Rule. And if English radicals and socialists had failed to exploit these convulsions to the full, that was hardly the fault of the Irish. Marx and O'Conner's point remained: Ireland was a wedge which could open the door to radical progress in Britain.

In the event, the rush through that door did not come, and history moved on down other corridors – towards the decisive years of 1912–21, whose ramifications for Ireland and for British socialists will be examined in the next chapter.

But first, a pertinent lesson of history from a century ago.

In the words of the English socialist newspaper *Justice*: 'England's difficulty is as old as Ireland's opportunity, and with Poland ever ready to revolt, we are discredited with the governments of other European nations whose despotic conduct we denounce.'

3.
Why Northern Ireland?

In December 1981 a young man called Peter Tatchell sent typewriters buzzing and cameras clicking in the dilapidated London borough of Bermondsey, where he had just been selected to stand as Labour Party candidate.

Tatchell was a left-winger, although not as left as many in the party, and he attempted to articulate his views in *London Labour Briefing*, the house journal of the metropolitan Labour Party left. In his article Tatchell advocated the use of 'extra-parliamentary' politics – for example, sit-down demonstrations in front of the Houses of Parliament. Although such proposals were hardly calculated to send shivers down the back of the British establishment, Tatchell's article led to his deselection as a candidate by the party leadership. This decision was later revoked, but by then the damage to Tatchell's reputation had been done, and he lost the subsequent by-election. It was a particularly sordid affair, not least because the victimisation was led by Michael Foot, who in his own youth had seemed eager to project the image of a one-person rent-a-crowd MP for any protest that was going. Foot defended his opposition to Tatchell in two articles in the *Observer* and went to some lengths to present himself as a guardian of parliamentary democracy, a system which, he insisted, might not be perfect, but *worked*. For a sometime historian this was a rather ingenuous view. Because, compared to some, Peter Tatchell was as staunch an upholder of parliamentarianism as the Speaker's Mace in the House of Commons. Take the following three statements, for instance.

> In our opposition to them we shall not be guided by the considerations, we shall not be restrained by the bonds, which would influence us in an ordinary political struggle. We shall use any means – whatever seems to us likely to be the most effective.
>
> There are things stronger than parliamentary majorities.
>
> They may tell us, if they like, that this is treason. It is not for men who have such stakes as we have at issue to trouble about the cost. We are prepared to take the consequences.

These statements were made, not in Chile in 1973, but in Britain in 1912, by Andrew Bonar Law and Edward Carson. At the time, Bonar Law was leader of the Conservative Party; Carson, a former Irish Solicitor General – and as such, an embodiment of official constitutionalism, law and order – was leader of the Irish Unionists. All the quotations refer to the Irish Home Rule controversy which was to rage for the next ten years. This controversy threw a harsh light on the current state of parliamentary democracy, for by the end of that period the wishes of the Irish majority and the votes of a majority in the House of Commons had been brushed aside as contemptuously as Chile's majority a half-century later. Those involved in this conspiracy included the leadership of the Conservative Party, the House of Lords, the King of Great Britain and Ireland, and the British military establishment. With protagonists like those, it was not simply a matter of a spot of civil disobedience in Parliament Square.

Accordingly, the history of this period is not only a crucial pointer to what was to follow in Ireland, it also has a bearing on something more general: namely, the belief of British social democrats that the only requirement for reform and progress is for the good guys to secure a majority in the House of Commons. It was on this assumption that the Labour Party was founded, and it was in defence of it that Peter Tatchell was victimised. Yet one glance at the Anglo-

Irish crisis of 1912–21 is enough to call every social democratic premise into question.

The origins of the crisis date back to the 1880s, when the Irish Parliamentary Party, led by Charles Parnell, won massive public support in Ireland for Home Rule. Popular endorsement of some form of Irish self-determination was nothing new, but this time the support extended into the ranks of the Liberal Party, under the leadership of William Gladstone, which seemed to suggest that Home Rule would eventually be granted. And although a split in the Liberal Party and opposition from the House of Lords robbed Gladstone of a victory on Home Rule, the Liberals were still committed to it when they returned to office in 1906. After the two 1910 elections, with the Liberals' parliamentary majority now dependent on the Irish Nationalists led by John Redmond, the third Home Rule Bill was introduced in parliament.

Considering the passions it aroused, the Bill was modest. It proposed the establishment of an Irish parliament with an upper and lower chamber so arranged as to give protection to Protestant interests in the North. Westminster was to retain control over foreign relations, war, and custom duties. The Irish police force was to remain under Westminster for six years. The power of the Home Rule parliament to raise taxes was to be limited, and as a symbol of the unity of the two islands, Ireland would continue to send MPs to Westminster, albeit in reduced numbers.

John Redmond, while accepting the Bill on the basis that it was as good as he could get, called it a 'provisional settlement', and this was how it was interpreted by all those with a finger in the Irish pie, except for the Liberal government. Unionist leader Edward Carson was particularly fearful of what could follow, and told a 50,000-strong 'parade' of Unionists in September 1911:

> We must be prepared, in the possible event of a Home Rule Bill passing, with such measures as will carry on for ourselves the government of these districts of which we have control. We must be prepared, the morning Home Rule passes, ourselves to become responsible

for the government of the Protestant province of Ulster.

This was not the evasive, all-things-to-all-people language most politicians employ. The rallying cry was open and undisguised: it was an incitement to rebellion. In passing, one might note that Carson's 'Protestant province of Ulster' was something of an exaggeration. Ulster, at that time made up of nine counties, had only a marginal Protestant majority. Three of its counties, Donegal, Monaghan and Cavan, had large Catholic majorities, Fermanagh and Tyrone had small Catholic majorities, and only in Down and Antrim was there a significant Protestant majority.

Such niceties did not stop Carson and his cohorts matching words with deeds. In September 1912 just under 500,000 Unionists signed the Ulster Covenant, which swore to use 'all necessary means' to 'defeat the present conspiracy to set up a Home Rule parliament in Ireland'. In January 1913 the Unionists' private army, the Ulster Volunteer Force, was established. In the following 18 months it paraded and drilled publicly, imported arms, and so became the first open manifestation of physical force in twentieth-century Ireland. Plans were made to set up a provisional government in Ulster, and Carson and his lieutenants even threatened to enter into an alliance with the German Kaiser.

This plot was not hatched in dark corners well away from the public gaze. On the contrary, the preparations for the coup d'état – for that is what it amounted to – were made in full view, and even boasted of in the House of Commons. Yet there were no arrests, no banishings to the Tower of London, no predecessors of the Special Air Services ordered in to give the rebels a short, sharp shock. Instead, the Liberal government looked on, occasionally scolded the conspirators, but did . . . nothing at all. The reason for this diffidence was encapsulated in one of the assurances Carson gave to his Ulster army: 'In the struggle we shall not be alone, because we have the best in England with us.'

That they were the best is arguable. For Carson it meant the gentlemen, the educated and pedigreed members of Bri-

Why Northern Ireland?

tish society – those who sat in the House of Lords, wrote leading articles in the *Times*, and held military, hereditary, and even royal titles. All of those who could lend the Ulster rebellion the authority it needed to succeed.

The revolt of 'England's best'

[...] top, there was the intervention of the recently
[...] George V. In May 1912 Tory leader Andrew
[...] informed the monarch of his royal duty.
[...] ie Liberals' Home Rule proposals, he said, it
[...] ve that His Majesty either dismiss the govern-
[...] e his assent to the Home Rule Bill. Although
[...] the constitutional rights to follow this advice,
[...] of action would have been politically seismic.
[...] that the royal veto had been brought to bear
[...] , during the reign of the Orange hero William
[...] -lag did not dissuade some influential oppo-
[...] ie Rule. Professor A.J. Dicey – a much lis-
[...] man in top Tory circles – agreed that the royal prerogative was 'an old and clumsy weapon', but insisted that 'we cannot afford to give it up.' Accordingly, Bonar Law and other leading Tories and Unionists, in audiences and through written submissions, urged King George to act. By the summer of 1913 the king was all but won over. In a letter of September that year he wrote to Prime Minister Asquith and warned the Liberal leader of the monarch's 'residual' right to dismiss the government.

Ultimately George V stepped back from the brink, but his last-minute caution did not alter the fact that he had come very close to behaving like a feudal monarch. More importantly, his refusal cannot disguise the breathtaking nature of the demands the Tories were making of him.

Equally dramatic was another ruse concocted by the Tory cabal – the spreading of military disaffection. For this particular extra-parliamentary tactic Bonar Law and Carson had the assistance of General Wilson, director of military operations in the War Office, General Paget, commander-in-chief of the army in Ireland, and General Gough, commander of the Third Cavalry Brigade. Carson started the mutiny ball rolling. In September 1913 he informed the government that the Unionists had 'pledges and promises from some of the greatest generals in the Army, who have given their word that, when the time comes, if it is necessary, they will come over and help us keep the old flag flying.' Two months later Bonar Law joined in with a history lesson which compared Prime Minister Asquith to James II in 1688: 'In order to carry out his despotic intentions the King had the largest Army which had ever been in England . . . there was a revolution and the King disappeared. Why? Because his own army refused to fight for him.'

With political leaders dropping such heavy hints, there was no shortage of army top brass able and willing to take them up on it. General Wilson was one. He served on a War Office committee which discussed how the army would be deployed in Ulster if the rebellion ever came to fruition. A fanatical Unionist, Wilson quickly relayed these discussions to Bonar Law, who in turn reported them to Carson.

General Paget took a more direct approach. At a meeting with his senior officers in Ireland in March 1914, he delivered a long tirade in which he attacked 'those swine' in the government, and encouraged officers in Ulster to 'disappear'. The officers in the rest of Ireland, said Paget, could not so easily disobey: they would have to move against the Unionists or face dismissal.

With the words of this rather exceptional military briefing ringing in his ears, one of Paget's officers, General Gough, decided to launch a pre-emptive strike. At the Curragh barracks near Dublin, Gough, his three colonels and 55 other officers declared that they would not move against the Unionists if instructed to do so. Although they offered to resign their commissions, the honourable public-school gesture could not disguise the bald mutiny of the act. Their boldness, however, was not matched by the government, who, faced with with this challenge to its authority, promptly capitulated. The mutineers received a written assurance that they would 'not be called on to enforce the Home Rule Bill in Ulster', and although this was later disavowed by Prime

Minister Asquith, the damage had already been done: the mutiny was successful, and the officers were allowed to retain their commissions.

The officers' reluctance to move against the Unionists was hardly surprising, for had they done so they could have come into conflict with the Ulster Volunteer Force, itself commanded and financed by the British military establishment's members and friends. Lieutenant-General Sir George Richardson, a veteran of many imperialist adventures, commanded the UVF. It was partly financed by the British League for the Support of Ulster, which also attempted to recruit former army officers to the cause. Among the 'best of British' who subscribed to this fund were Waldorf Astor, Lord Rothschild, Lord Iveagh, the Duke of Bedford, and Rudyard Kipling.

Against such pillars of the establishment, as well as the Tory Party, the army, and the House of Lords, Asquith's alliance – the Liberals, John Redmond's nationalists, and the majority of the House of Commons – caved in. In March 1914, when Redmond agreed to the 'temporary' exclusion of Ulster from the domain of Home Rule, it was the beginning of partition. It was also the beginning of the end of John Redmond. The next step in his downward slide was taken at the outbreak of the First World War, when he acted as a recruiting sergeant in Ireland for the British Army, and the end itself came in the Easter of 1916, when the Republican Rising swallowed up the constitutional moderation he had promoted for so long. But if extremists were to blame for the death of Redmondism, they were not Irish at all, but British. It was the right-wing extremists and their counter-revolution who opened the door to the Irish revolutionaries, so that in later years the inheritors of the Rising, Sinn Fein, could point to 1912–14 and persuade the Irish majority with some ease that polite lobbying in the Commons was as useless as it was demeaning.

Of the notables who had set this chain of events in motion, Bonar Law went on to become prime minister, and Generals Wilson and Gough served their country in the First World War, demonstrating in the course of their duties a bloody incompetence which sent tens of thousands to unnecessary deaths. Wilson later became a Unionist MP, while Edward Carson, who had proclaimed rebellion against Britain so vehemently, ended up in the British War Cabinet. Thus the British establishment not only protected its own political criminals, but even promoted them.

One Vladimir Ilyich, soon to be known to the world as Lenin, was quietly observing it all. In the aftermath of the Curragh mutiny he wrote of 'an epoch-making turning-point, the day when the noble landowners of Britain tore the British constitution and British law to shreds and gave an excellent lesson in class struggle.'

Partition

After the First World War, the lesson continued. On 14 December 1918, the general election results unambiguously relayed the mood of the Irish majority. Of the 105 Irish seats at Westminster, Sinn Fein won 73, the old parliamentary nationalists won six, and the Unionists took 26. Even in the North a majority voted for Irish independence, with the Unionists winning a majority in only four of the nine Ulster counties. In the six north-east counties the nationalist Republican minority was far larger than the Unionists' minority in Ireland as a whole. There was no disguising the popular mandate for Sinn Fein: few British political parties, before or since, have been so massively supported at an election.

In Britain the election saw the return of the Coalition government, led by the Liberal David Lloyd George but dominated by the Tories and Unionists. With this political coloration the cabinet was hardly likely to show Irish democracy much sympathy. At the end of 1919, when Lloyd George announced his terms for an Irish settlement, they were essentially the old Home Rule solution. The main departure from the 1912 Bill was the proposal to partition Ireland into two parliaments, each subservient to Westminster. The partition was to be permanent.

The new Sinn Fein MPs were not at the House to hear

Why Northern Ireland?

Lloyd George's scheme, for over half of them were in British prisons, and the others, true to their electoral promises, were refusing to recognise Westminister's right to rule Ireland. Instead, they unilaterally established an independent Irish parliament in Dublin: the Dail.

The Unionists were in a quandary. For some, like Carson, the Ulster rebellion had only been a means to an end – the building of a British outpost in Ireland whose strength would block all possibilities of Home Rule. Lloyd George's proposals fell short of this aim, but because Carson had based his campaign in Ulster it was hard for him then to argue with the government's definition of Ulster as a separate and distinct province. He advised the Unionists not to vote against the Bill, advice which they followed – but they did not vote *for* it, either. And so the partition of Ireland was achieved without any support from its people's elected representatives. It was a dictate from the British government.

For the boundaries of the new state the Unionists would have preferred the nine counties of Ulster. But the political balance within that area between Unionists and nationalists would have been too precarious to guarantee the Unionists permanent control; accordingly, they opted for the six North-east counties. There was no cultural, geographic, economic or political rationale for the delineation of this new state of Northern Ireland. It was established via a sectarian head-count which included just enough Catholics to make the new state viable, but not enough to endanger its long-term future.

As 1920 progressed control over the rest of Ireland became the main issue at stake. Two contemporary accounts summarised the situation. Said the Labour Party:

> It is undeniable that Sinn Fein stands for the ideal of an Irish Republic. It does, in fact, claim that the Irish Republic is already in being, and that its Dail Eireann is its parliament. It is also undeniable that in some directions, Sinn Fein functions as a de facto government. It has established courts whose decisions are respected, and issues decrees that are obeyed by a

considerable part of the population. Its authority, unlike that of the English government, is derived from the consent of the majority of the Irish electors who voted at the last election. It has created departments and appointed ministers . . . All these activities are declared illegal and unconstitutional; they are in form and effect a declaration of independence.

And the fledgeling Communist Party:

> Bit by bit the British administrative institutions were replaced by and administered through the Dail . . . This struggle in reality led to open war . . . Viewing it as a civil war, the British government drafted in troops, organised their 'black and tan' murdering and plundering brigades, suppressed free speech and the press . . . Viewing the struggle as a national war and looking upon England as an alien invader the Irish set up their institutions in order to drive the imperialist usurper from the land.

The Communist Party's allegations of murder and plundering were true. Certainly the Irish, organised in the Irish Republican Army, did not eschew ruthlessness, although their guns were by and large directed against the British security forces and their agents. British reprisals, on the other hand, both unofficial and official, were deliberately extended to the non-combatant sections of the population.

If the military tactics of the two sides were markedly different, there was an even more telling contrast between the promptness of the moves to suppress the Irish revolt, and the tolerance shown by the British government to the Ulster rebels of 1912–14. Indeed, during the Irish War of Independence the old Ulster Volunteer Force was reorganised – with the blessing of the British government, which released Lieutenant-Colonel Spender from his post at the Ministry of Pensions to the more pressing work of arming the Unionists. Three months later, in October 1920, the government announced the formation of the Ulster Special Constabulary, which was the UVF under another name, and recognised as such in cabinet discussions. The USC was entirely made up of Protestants.

The Anglo-Irish Treaty

The other Irish rebels – those who reflected the political allegiances of the majority of the population – remained at war with the British until the end of 1921. The strength of the resistance forced the government to the conference table in December of that year, but once negotiations began the Irish proved no match for perfidious Albion. Lloyd George bluffed, threatened, set seductive traps, and eventually promised the Irish negotiators a 'total' and 'terrible' war if they did not sign away the Republic they had been pledged to defend. Without reference to Dublin, they signed. The terms they had accepted included the right of Britain to use Irish naval ports, an oath of allegiance to the Crown from the 'Home Rule' parliament, and partition along the lines proposed in the 1920 Government of Ireland Bill.

In private, Lloyd George told the Irish delegates that a boundary commission which would review the frontiers of the Northern state would trim two-and-a-half counties from 'Ulster', thus making it untenable. He also promised a Council of Ireland, which was to open the way to the reunification of Ireland. The boundary commission finally met five years later, and broke up in disarray with the majority endorsing the existing borders. The Council of Ireland never met. In the South of Ireland a civil war was fought over the terms of the Treaty, with the British helping the pro-Treaty forces to victory. In Britain, Lloyd George proclaimed the Treaty 'the greatest day in the history of the British Empire'. In the House of Commons J.R.Clynes of the Labour Party declared: 'The Labour Party rejoices.'

For Ireland, North and South, the years ahead were to testify to the instability engendered by the Treaty. The 'carnival of reaction' which James Connolly had predicted would follow partition was duly opened. The aborted Irish national revolution was to dominate the politics and consciousness of working people on both sides of the blood-stained border.

It could be argued, of course, that the consequences of

the Anglo-Irish Treaty and of partition, while an obvious preoccupation for Irish socialists, is of only peripheral interest to those outside the fractured 32 counties – unfortunate for Ireland's left, perhaps, but hardly a reason why contemporary Ireland should be a fundamental concern of socialists in general. But to argue thus would be to neglect the lessons of 1912–21. To summarise what happened: a majority in the House of Commons was overruled and challenged militarily by a powerful and dominating section of the British ruling class. Those who led this rebellion were not penalised but rewarded by the parliamentary democracy they had defied. By contrast, the wishes of the Irish majority were denied and suppressed by force of arms and the civilian minority in Ireland who supported this suppression were themselves equipped and organised by the British government. Finally, the Irish majority faced the threat of a genocidal war.

That was how Britain's 'parliamentary democracy' conducted itself in those critical years. The lesson is as loud as an Orangeman's drum: if needs be, the rich and powerful sections of a democracy will use every weapon at their disposal to overturn a popular majority, whether it is expressed inside or outside parliamentary debating chambers.

The 'carnival of reaction'

It may be said that what the British ruling class did to the Irish over 60 years ago is all water under the bridge. In the first place, this is not how the Irish see it, and it is the Irish who have had to live with the deformed offspring of that marriage between North-east Irish Unionism and the British ruling class which calls itself Northern Ireland. Moreover, it would be very naive to assume that history could not be repeated, and that the political banditry of the British ruling class was an aberration peculiar to 1912–21. For, in 1971, Brigadier Frank Kitson, commanding the British Army in Belfast, wrote:

> In a democratic country it is the duty of soldiers to know how to wage war in any of its forms, and it is the duty of the people to elect representatives who will

> only make war when it is right to do so. When conflicts
> occur, soldiers, like other people, have to have faith in
> the moral rectitude of their government to some extent
> . . . But if any man, soldier or civilian, is convinced
> that his country is wrong he should cease to support it
> and take the consequences.

And this is what Andrew Sefton, a British Army officer stationed in Belfast, had to say about the army's relations with the loyalist paramilitary Ulster Defence Association during their strike in 1974:

> The army chose, quite deliberately, to give the UDA
> tacit support. The UDA virtually ran East and North
> Belfast . . . The army has shown that it is not
> prepared to act in certain circumstances . . . For the
> first time, the army decided that it was right and that it
> knew best and the politicians had better toe the line.

But the sheer scale of British Army defiance of an elected government has not been repeated in the Irish crisis of present times. One explanation for this might be that there is not the same sympathy for the loyalists among the British ruling class as there was earlier in the century. Also, the political aims of today's loyalists, army and successive British governments are one and the same – defence of the Northern Ireland state – so there is no need for army chiefs to rebel against government orders. Which is not to say, however, that such a contingency might not arise in the future.

Other comparisons can be made between 1912–21 and the era ushered in by the events of 1969. In the earlier period, the normal principles which are supposed to inform the application of 'law and order' in a parliamentary democracy were dispensed with. Similarly, from 1969 onwards Britain jailed Irish Republicans, and also some loyalists, without trial, and shot down unarmed demonstrators, including a fair number of children; Britain abolished trial by jury for those suspected of what the Prevention of Terrorism Acts labelled 'violence for political ends'; Britain proscribed the IRA while permitting its loyalist counterpart, the UDA, to continue, and in general administered a rule of law which has drawn condemnation from the European

Court of Human Rights, Amnesty International and the National Council for Civil Liberties – to name but a few of the humanitarian groups who have spoken out publicly against it.

This record alone should demonstrate why the Northern Ireland of today is important for British socialists. Furthermore, understanding how and why Northern Ireland was born raises enormous implications for socialists everywhere. One need only look at Lloyd George insisting in September 1921 that the demands of the Irish majority as expressed through Sinn Fein must not be met: 'Suppose we give in to them . . . it will lower the prestige and dignity of this country . . . it will give the impression that we have lost grip, that the Empire has no further force, and will have an effect in India and throughout Europe.'

The 'we' in question were those who ran and profited from the British Empire; the 'them' in this case were the Irish, but equally could have been the Egyptians during the 1956 Suez crisis, the Kenyans in the 1950s, the miners during the premiership of Edward Heath, or the Argentinians during the Falklands/Malvinas campaign. Ireland of 1912–21 is not just a relic of history or a criminal episode in Britain's imperial past; it is an object lesson applicable to all political climates.

In contemporary Ireland, the most assiduous students of this lesson are in the Provisional Republican movement. The conclusions they have drawn from their studies will now be examined.

4.
The Republicans

On 29 July 1982, *An Phoblacht/Republican News*, the newspaper of the Provisional Republican movement, fired the verbal equivalent of an Armalite rifle. The target was the British far left:

> The long-awaited socialist revolution in Britain, planned for Wednesday last week, July 21st, unfortunately had to be called off because of the IRA bomb attack against British soldiers in London the previous day.
>
> This at least is what two of the main British lefty newspapers would have us believe in their condemnation of the successful attack.
>
> Both the daily *News Line* – voice of the Workers' Revolutionary Party – and *Socialist Worker* – weekly organ of the party of that name – carried very similar editorials.
>
> They both claimed that the Thatcher government, tottering under the weight of three million unemployed, the hospital workers' strike, gay policemen and intruders at the Palace, Russian spies in communications and corruption at Scotland Yard, was only awaiting a touch from the revolutionary British proletariat to collapse and be replaced by the workers' state.
>
> The IRA, by drawing attention to the fact that the British have been battering and butchering the Irish 'proletariat' for centuries, 'distracted' media attention from all this and saved the Thatcher government!

> ... These lunatics of the British left hope to return to the safe haven of their trendy middle-class talk shops, organise their pickets of the Israeli embassy in support of faraway Palestine, have sing-along evenings for faraway El Salvadoreans and consider boycotts against faraway South Africans.
>
> At the same time the fact that the government of their country is waging a long and bloody imperialist war on their own doorstep is a 'distraction'.
>
> Buggery at Buckingham Palace is, for these British lefties, a more revolutionary situation than Butchery in the Bogside.

It is clear, then, that relations between the British left and Irish Republicans are not always amicable, even when the left groups involved consider themselves revolutionary, and have on occasions expressed their sympathy with the IRA. And if the SWP and the WRP drew such salvoes from *An Phoblacht/Republican News*, one wonders what sort of polemical missiles would be required for a debate with the British Labour Party or the Communist Party of Great Britain.

The violent past

The Provisional IRA has yet to become fashionable with British socialists. It is easy to romanticise about guns and bombs when they are directed against dictators in Latin America or Uncle Sam in South-East Asia. When they are employed in Northern Ireland – which for all its faults does not ban trade unions and does, for most of the time, tolerate peaceful protest – then violence for political ends is a different kettle of fish. Even more so when the Provisionals leave their own backyard and plant bombs in London or Birmingham. What, people ask, has the British public done to deserve that? Surely it is the duty of socialists to condemn such acts?

A self-styled 'Irish émigré' in London, writing in 1799, had this to say:

> It is always a bad undertaking in a private individual to become the advocate of a suffering people. It is

particularly difficult at this present moment to be the
advocate of the people of Ireland, because there are
among them men who have taken the power of redress
into their own hands, and committed acts of outrage.
. . . The system to which the Castle [British
administration in Ireland] has resorted to silence
murmur, has produced outrage – the measures which
they took to punish outrage have created conspiracy,
assassination, and in many instances, treason.
Throughout the whole process of discontent . . . the
administration were the aggressors and the
irregularities which have followed were but the
reaction of a high and irritable spirit in the people,
compressed by coercion which left no vent to its
feelings but in acts of private and public violence.

British radicals have concurred with this view. In October 1819 the *Cap of Liberty* insisted: 'If any country in this world has stronger reasons than another for asserting her independence *vi et armis* that country is Ireland.' Fifty years later the radical Charles Bradlaugh, who did not even support Irish independence, commented on the Fenian Brotherhood's pledge to expel Britain forcibly from Ireland:

But why does Fenianism appeal to force? Is it not
because by successive governments, empty promise
after empty promise has been made of attempt at
redressal of Ireland's grievances, and all have been
broken? . . . It is you, the governing classes, who
have set the Irish race the bad example of the appeal to
force. You have ruled them by force.

Even later, in 1920, the British Socialist Party, forerunner of the Communist Party, maintained:

We are exhorted to condemn the wild acts of Irish
desperadoes. We are harrowed by tales of midnight
shootings and murders. And the appeal leaves us
unmoved. For we remember other things. The tanks
patrolling Irish roads, for instance; the groups of
English soldiery decked out in all the paraphernalia of
war, and full of horrible potentialities of massacre; the
executions of 1916. Like causes produce like effects,

and oppression breeds outrage with the inevitability of a law of nature.

The reasoning used, in terms of cause and effect, would be familiar to any O-level history pupil. It is important to establish that there is a socialist/radical tradition in Britain – albeit a minority one – which has been capable of placing Irish 'terrorism' within this logical framework.

The violent present

The suggestion could be made that even if one accepts that the Irish nationalists of the past were justified in using physical force, this need not mean that the same applies today, or that the Irish struggle is powered by the same motor.

At this point, applying some of the above arguments to modern times might be instructive. According to the 1799 tract quoted above, the British were the aggressors, and Irish violence merely a reaction. It is also the case that neither the Provisional IRA nor any other armed Republican group was operative in August 1969 when British troops were deployed on the streets of Northern Ireland. In fact, the Provisionals were born out of the very defencelessness of the Catholic working-class ghettos attacked by the 'B' Specials and the loyalist mobs in Belfast that summer. And although the Provisionals had begun their military campaign by the summer of 1971, it was the internment without trial of Republicans and socialists which began in August that produced the real escalation in Republican violence. The alternative – peaceful protest – was effectively ruled out in January 1972, when the British Army shot down 14 unarmed demonstrators on the streets of Derry on 'Bloody Sunday'. Indeed, throughout the 1970s and the early 1980s, the best recruiting sergeant for the IRA was – to put it mildly – the over-enthusiasm of the British security forces. The torture of internees in 1971, the torture of Republican suspects in the police barracks of Castlereagh, and Gough in Armagh in the late 1970s, the treatment of Republican H Block prisoners in Long Kesh from 1976 to 1981 – all these events fed the rivers of Catholic resentment in which the IRA swam.

The first bomb in Britain, planted by the Official IRA at the barracks of the Parachute Regiment in Aldershot, was intended as a reprisal for Bloody Sunday. As the pamphleteer of 1799 would have put it, violence begets violence.

Another historical argument can be brought to bear on the present. Charles Bradlaugh cited the broken promises of the British government as a root cause of the 1867 Fenian Uprising. Once again, this was a feature of British policy from 1968 onwards. The restrictions on civil liberties contained in the Unionists' Special Powers Act were revoked from 1969 to 1972, but they were replaced by the constraints of the Prevention of Terrorism Act, which Home Secretary Roy Jenkins himself described as 'draconian', and the Emergency Provisions Act. As Harold Wilson had promised in 1969, the 'B' Specials were disbanded – only to be replaced by the Ulster Defence Regiment, which soon became equally unacceptable to Catholics because of its loyalist prejudices. And even though the civil rights demand of 'one man, one vote' for council elections was granted, the powers of local councils were trimmed; meanwhile, in loyalist-dominated councils, anti-Catholic discrimination in employment continued, a fact underlined by numerous reports, some of which were drawn up by government agencies. The overall unemployment figure for Catholics also failed to improve, with three times as many of them on the dole as Protestants throughout the 1970s. All these factors, then, suggest that it is not the case that the Provisionals did not give the 'reforms' a chance. Rather, the failure of the reforms gave the Provisionals their chance.

The way they seized their opportunity had nothing in common with the tactics and strategy of British social democracy. However, on the occasions when the Provisionals or their supporters did bow to electoral convention, they were given little encouragement by the British government. After Bobby Sands, the Provisional hunger striker, won the Fermanagh and South Tyrone by-election in April 1981, the Thatcher government changed the rules of the electoral game to prevent other prisoners standing in Sands's place when he died. When leading Provisional

Gerry Adams and four other Sinn Fein candidates won seats in the Northern Ireland Assembly in the summer of 1982, Northern Ireland Secretary James Prior immediately declared that on no account would he meet or discuss with these duly elected public representatives. All five were subsequently banned from entering Britain.

In contrast, one might take note of the occasions when the British government did enter direct negotiations with the IRA – in 1972 when the Republican military campaign was at a peak, and in 1974 just after the Birmingham bombings. The Provisionals could hardly be blamed for concluding that if they wanted to influence the British, election successes were nothing compared to the power which came from the barrel of a gun.

Irish Republicans had reached such conclusions before. British premier William Gladstone admitted that it was the Fenian Uprising of 1867 which persuaded him to attempt land reform in Ireland; when this failed and sections of the Irish peasantry began to use more forceful methods to drive out the landlords, Gladstone was converted to Home Rule. And again in 1921, it was the Irish War of Independence which forced the British into negotiations with Sinn Fein, and won for the South of Ireland a semi-autonomy. The harsh truth is that violence from the Irish has evoked a response from the British, whereas peaceful methods of protest tend to be greeted with indifference.

Seen in this context, the methods of the Provisionals appear more a product than a source of Irish contemporary history. Rather than criticising the tactics of Repulicanism, then, a more pertinent approach might be to examine its political ideology.

Nationalism and socialism

The crux of the British left's argument with the Provisionals is the primary significance they attach to the struggle for a 32-county Ireland. Nothing to do with class, say the British; and, furthermore, nationalism in any form must be rejected by socialists: 'the proletariat has no country,' in Marx's words.

However, it was also Marx who pointed out, particularly in his writings on Ireland, that socialists must differentiate between the nationalism of colonial and imperialist powers and the nationalism of those they oppress. The relationship between socialism and national self-determination is an issue which at least some British socialists have tried to tackle. In November 1920 the executive of the newly formed Communist Party of Great Britain declared:

> A nation is being murdered under our eyes . . . There are Communists who say . . . it is not our concern. This is a nationalist struggle . . . we are internationalists . . . In such a case as Ireland . . . the case of a small nation being held in forcible suppression by a great imperialist power – the national struggle and the class struggle are inseparable from one another. The struggle against imperialism for national independence is a necessary phase of the struggle against capitalism for the workers' independence . . .
>
> The Republican movement is essentially a working-class movement. There are, it is true, middle-class men as well as bourgeois, by the chance of birth, in its ranks. But they do not mould it. They are being moulded by it. The strength and vigour and inspiration of the movement lies in the workers and workers' organisations . . . Even those who are not communists or socialists of any kind have some vision that their job is not merely the ousting of the English government, but the overthrow of the English system – which is the capitalist system. And the workers themselves see in the establishment of the Irish Republic the first step – the necessary first step – to the establishment of the Irish Workers' Republic.

But how true was this of Irish Republicanism in 1920? and how true is it today? What exactly *is* the ideology of Irish Republicanism?

If there is no single answer to these questions, it is because there is no unitary tradition within the movement for Irish self-determination. Consider, for instance, Padraic Pearse, the leader of the 1916 Easter Rising which proclaimed the Irish Republic half a century before the Provisionals. While Pearse emphasised the need for Ireland to have 'spiritual and intellectual independence, as well as political independence', it was above all the 'spiritual' aspect he insisted on. He did not see the Easter Rising in terms of anti-imperialism or class struggle. This sort of materialism was anathema to Pearse, for, as he believed: 'Freedom, being a spiritual necessity, transcends all corporeal necessities.' There were times when Pearse defined Irish national sovereignty as including control of the nation's material resources, but more often he placed Irish nationalism within a metaphysical framework. Nationality was a 'nation's soul', which could only be redeemed by blood sacrifice. A character in a play Pearse wrote speaks for the author's conception of the Easter Rising: 'One man can free a people, as one man redeemed the world. I will take my pike, I will go into battle with bare hands. I will stand up . . . as Christ hung naked before men on a tree.'

Just what, one might ask, has this mumbo-jumbo in common with scientific socialism? 'Was Pearse a socialist?' asks one contemporary writer, and goes on to decide that 'he had a definite social conscience . . . he was influenced by Fintan Lalor, a revolutionary socialist. Pearse was in the radical Republican tradition . . . As a radical and progressive thinker he was developing his ideas on the need for social revolution.' But the answer, by implication, is no. Pearse was a radical, yes; moving towards socialism just before he was executed, yes – but certainly not an out-and-out socialist. This regretful verdict came, interestingly enough, from Gerry Adams, one of the leading members of the Provisional Republican movement. In other words, one of Republicanism's foremost representatives of the 1970s was criticising one of its patron saints for not being a thoroughgoing socialist. The criticism is made between the lines, but it is there all the same.

If Republicanism is no monolithic ideology, even less so is the ideology of the broader Irish nationalist movement, in whose ranks some of the fiercest political battles have been fought.

Socialists and nationalism

James Connolly, in *Labour and Irish History*, mounts an unrestrained polemical attack on what he termed 'bourgeois nationalism'. As a critique of aspects of Irish nationalism, it has rarely been bettered, and as an example of how differently Irish independence was conceived by the wide range of its supporters, it could hardly be clearer. It is worth quoting at length:

> Hence the spokesmen of the middle class . . . have consistently sought . . . the denial of all relations between the social rights of the Irish toilers and the political rights of the Irish nation. It was hoped and intended by these means to create what is termed 'a real national movement', i.e. a movement in which each class would recognise the rights of the other classes, and laying aside their contentions would unite in a national struggle against the common enemy – England. Needless to say, the only class deceived by such phrases was the working class. The bourgeois press and politicians incessantly strive to inflame the working-class mind to fever heat upon questions outside the range of their own class interests. War, religion, race, language, political reform, patriotism – apart from whatever intrinsic merits they possess – all serve in the hands of counter-irritants, whose function is to avoid the catastrophe of social revolution by engendering heat in such parts of the body politic as are farthest removed from the seat of economic enquiry . . .
>
> During the last hundred years every generation in Ireland has witnessed an attempted rebellion against English rule. Every such conspiracy or rebellion has drawn the majority of its adherents from the lower orders in town and country, yet under the inspiration of a few middle-class doctrinaires the social question

has been rigorously excluded from the field of action to be covered by the rebellion in the hope that by such exclusion it would be possible to conciliate the upper classes and enlist them in the struggle for freedom.

This, then, is one aspect of the Irish national movement – that it can be used to smother class differences within Ireland. But, as Connolly's participation in the Easter Rising suggests, there is another side to it. A week before going into battle in 1916, Connolly advised the soldiers of the Irish Citizen Army: 'In the event of victory, hold on to your rifles, as those with whom we are fighting may stop before our goal is reached. We are out for economic as well as political liberty.' Therein lies another strand of the Irish nationalist story, and a good reason why socialists should participate in it – to infuse it with socialist politics, and, perhaps even more important, to conduct a 'class struggle' within it.

There has always been some kind of class-struggle wing within the Irish national movement. *Labour in Irish History* is an account of this tendency, and of its leaders. Connolly records the efforts of William Thompson, 'a forerunner of Marx', in the 1820s; the 'socialist teachings' of John Mitchel and Fintan Lalor in the 1840s; the 'militant class feeling' expressed by some of the Fenian leaders in the 1860s; the 'social war' conducted by the Land League in the 1870s and 80s. The militancy of these leaders and movements was not confined to social and economic issues; it also extended to the national struggle, and to a degree that often brought them into conflict with the more constitutional leaders of the national movement. Yet they did not counterpose social and economic agitation to the struggle for self-determination; rather, they saw it as the highest expression of nationalism, the only way Pearse's 'sovereign people' could become *truly* sovereign.

Another aspect of this class-struggle tendency in Irish nationalism is, paradoxical though it may sound, its internationalism. This tradition dates back to the very beginning of Irish Republicanism, to Theobald Wolfe Tone and the 1798

United Irishmen Rising which he led. Based on Tom Paine's *Rights of Man*, the United Irishmen manifesto resolved to work with 'the Jacobin Club of Paris, the Revolutionary Society in England, the Committee for Reform in Scotland', and its central message was as follows:

> When the aristocracy come forward, the people fall backward; when the people come forward, the aristocracy, fearful of being left behind, insinuate themselves into our ranks and rise into timid leaders or treacherous auxiliaries. They mean to make us their instruments; let us rather make them our instruments . . . On the 14th July, the day that shall ever commemorate the French Revolution, let this society pour out their first libation to European liberty, eventually, the liberty of the world.

This is not the inward-looking, sterile 'Mother-Ireland' nationalism often attributed to the heirs of Wolfe Tone. Nor was Tone exceptional in placing his Republicanism within the wider European context. The Young Irelanders, who led something of a fiasco of a rebellion in 1849, drew their inspiration from the Europe-wide radical movement which had fired the revolutions on the continent in 1848. And over a century after Tone had hoped his rebellion would ignite others in Europe, James Connolly looked on the 1916 Rising as one which could 'set the torch to a European conflagration that will not burn out until the last throne and the last capitalist bond and debenture will be shrivelled in the funeral pyre of the last war-lord.'

To say that there has always been a democratic and internationalist strand within Irish Republicanism does not necessarily make it socialist. What it does is allow a socialist element to exist within it, and, potentially, to dominate it.

But is this simply a historical observation, or does it also apply to the ideology and practice of modern Republicanism as represented by the Provisionals? Can one even think of applying adjectives like 'democratic', 'international' or 'socialist' to an organisation so persistently reviled by mass media and politicians alike?

The Provisionals

When it was formed in January 1970, Provisional Sinn Fein was a conservative face of Irish Republicanism. One of the reasons the Provisionals gave for splitting from the Official Republican movement was the 'extreme socialism' of the Officials; they later went on to claim that the Officials were plotting to set up 'an ultra-left-wing front' which 'diverted the Republican movement to political and social agitation to the almost total exclusion of the traditional military role.' Twelve years later the Provisional IRA was delivering a very different message. Their 1982 Easter greeting, quoted below, summarises what the Provisionals currently purport to stand for:

> The lesson – an age-old one in Ireland – is clear for those who wish to see it. The 'stake in the country' people, those whose interests coincide in the long run with British interests were, and are, never for the Republic or the Republican struggle . . .
>
> As it is, both major conservative groupings in the twenty-six counties [Fianna Fail, Fine Gael] govern their part of Ireland in the interests of the five per cent who control 71 per cent of Irish wealth. The Irish ruling class has more in common with the British ruling class than with its own working class. The common interests are manifest not only in the living conditions of our people but, of course, in the continued existence of partition and support for the Western Alliance [NATO] . . .
>
> Republican resistance must be waged on all fronts, and while the struggle is much more difficult in twenty-six-county terms, nonetheless it must be pursued intelligently with all the vigour at our disposal. We must, as a movement, become involved in people's struggles. We must be active Republicans in our locality, fusing together local campaigns with the unresolved national question. To concentrate on one aspect of British imperialism – the military occupation of the six counties – is insufficient if in doing so we

ignore the other issues more directly affecting our people. That those grievances are caused by the lack of national sovereignty and the lack of real control by ordinary people over their own lives is irrelevant to most people, and will remain so unless Republicans strive to correct and educate in their own areas, in their workplaces and among their neighbours. This can only be accomplished by a real involvement in people's affairs.

In the six counties as well, there is a belated need for a conscious Republican involvement in the issues which affect ordinary people. The Republican base in the six counties must be widened to take in more than military resistance to British Troops and the loyalist RUC and UDR. Republicans must be involved with the people we profess to lead in their everyday struggles for better housing and against poverty and unemployment . . .

We take this opportunity to once again re-emphasise our commitment to the complete destruction of British rule in Ireland by the Irish people. We demand the immediate and complete withdrawal of British troops as a first step in this process.

Only through armed struggle will we be listened to, only through the struggle waged by the men and women of the IRA can we win national freedom and end division and sectarianism in Ireland . . .

Republicans remain determined, as always, to secure conditions in which the people of this country will unite in a thirty-two-county democratic, socialist republic. Nothing else will suffice. Nothing else will be accepted.

This suggests that the Provisionals' politics have evolved considerably since 1970, and towards the left. The leftward turn is indicated also by a 1982 booklet produced by the Provisionals, called *Notes for Revolutionaries* and described as 'notes, quotes, poems and songs on aspects of revolutionary struggle and ideology'. James Connolly, Wolfe Tone, Fintan Lalor and other Republican heroes are quoted in the booklet, but they are outnumbered by their international counterparts, among them Emma Goldman, Alexandra Kollontai, Che Guevara, Sitting Bull, Mao Tse-tung, Antonio Gramsci, John MacLean, George Jackson, General Giap, John Reed, Lenin, Trotsky, Kwame Nkrumah, Malcolm X and Bertolt Brecht. An Irish priest is also quoted, but with ridicule rather than approval. His remark reads: 'It is a sure sign of the break-up of the planet when women take to leaving their homes and coming out in public.' Not only do the heartless granite-faced men of the IRA have ideological links with international terrorists, then, but they also threaten to have a sense of humour.

The booklet also contains a clue to the Provisionals' leftward swing. Ruairi O Bradaigh, Sinn Fein president, is quoted as saying:

> No one phase of [the Irish] struggle has gone on for so long. It is not simply the exhausting effort of a single generation, for within the present struggle the turnover of the generation has already taken place. A new generation is setting the pace now.

There is an implied irony in the choice of this quotation, for in the internal ideological struggle which has gone on since 1970, O Bradaigh is very much a member of the old guard, a conservative 1970s Provo as opposed to the radical Provos of the 1980s.

The latter only won control of the entire Irish Republican movement after the Sinn Fein conference of November 1983. They had gained the leadership of the IRA some time before that. Here it is important to draw a distinction between the IRA and Sinn Fein, for it is not true that they are one and the same, as British propagandists insist. There is, for example, a geographic difference. Sinn Fein has invariably been run from the South of Ireland, whereas the IRA has, of necessity, been run from the North, where the military battle is primarily being waged.

The experience of that battle, and of the general struggle which has taken place on the streets of Belfast, Derry and elsewhere has affected the combatants deeply. For the very first time in the long history of Irish Republicanism most of its military campaign has been fought in working-class areas by working-class people. This proletarianisation of the IRA has been reproduced politically. The IRA spring from the Catholic working-class ghettos of Northern Ireland, and, for its contemporary leaders, the real reason for the 1970 split from the Officials was less to avoid 'extreme socialism' than to make sure that the Catholic working-class community would never again be as defenceless as they were in August 1969, when the Officials' guns were lost, buried, or sold to the Free Wales Army.

This sense of attachment to the Catholic working-class ghettos has allowed the modern IRA to exist within them. And their loyalty has been reciprocated, as was clear in the 1982 Northern Ireland Assembly elections, when Gerry Adams topped the poll in West Belfast, and four other Sinn Fein candidates were elected from working-class constituencies. The results sent a shock-wave through polite liberal circles in Britain, but to those who had paid any attention to the ebb and flow of political affiliations in Northern Ireland since 1968, they came as no surprise at all. The really significant fact was that the Provisionals had at last displayed the wit to test their support electorally. That support was in evidence again in the 1983 general election when Adams won West Belfast, and Sinn Fein became the most popularly supported party in Catholic working-class constituencies. Some may still query how tens of thousands of ordinary folk can vote for representatives who have the taint of bomb-planting and all manner of blood-letting. The simple answer is that there are no 'ordinary folk' in the Catholic ghettos of Northern Ireland. Ordinary folk do not experience the denial of civil rights, internment without trial, Bloody Sunday, curfews and torture. Ordinary folk do not see their children killed by plastic or even lead bullets, or live in a community occupied by what they see as foreign troops. Add to this the commoner characteristics of advanced capitalism – unemployment, bad housing, wretched social services – and you have an everyday tale of 'ordinary' Catholic folk.

Some observers – particularly those of loyalist persuasion – would object that the Catholics have brought all this on themselves, but the Catholics can hardly be expected to agree. So they cheer when those they see as responsible for their plight – the British – are gunned down or blown up, and they vote for those who pull the triggers. To outsiders, it may not be acceptable behaviour, but surely it is understandable.

The Provisionals are not just representatives of Catholic working-class reaction against the British. Very often they are also the leaders of working-class communities. The most class-conscious of those leaders have been cautious in their attempts to politicise both the Republican movement and its constituency. The Provisionals have not suddenly lurched to the left under the direction of the young red guard in Belfast. The transformation of green to green and red has been a slow a subtle shading, and is not yet complete. For instance, Sinn Fein has been heavily criticised by some on the British left for a reluctance to thrust women's liberation to the centre of its politics, and an unwillingness to take a stand on issues like the lack of availability of contraception and abortion in the South of Ireland. And it is true that for a long time Sinn Fein leaders tried to avoid such controversies for fear of alienating their more conservative supporters in the South. But on this, too, their stance has changed. When the 1983 referendum on abortion was held in the South, Sinn Fein – prodded by radical women in its ranks – publicly argued against making abortion unconstitutional.

There is no doubt that a tangible shift has taken place, and however political theorists define the Provisionals – as Republican, socialist, marxist, petty-bourgeois nationalist, or a mixture of all four – it is hard to refute the proposition that there is no organisation in western Europe as far to the left as the Provisionals which can still boast their kind of mass support. Marxists who complain of the Provisionals' lack of programmatic clarity should bear this in mind. Left social democrats who raise the totem of the people's will should ask themselves when they last enjoyed the kind of warm, emotional support that Bobby Sands, Gerry Adams and their colleagues received from their working-class constituencies.

At this stage it is not possible to give a definitive political classification of the Provisionals because it is an organisation which is evolving, and no one can be sure where that evolution will cease. But a plea can be made to the British left not to judge the Provisionals on the basis of its own tactics, strategy or obsessions, and, instead, to remember the wisdom of Connolly's remark that 'each nation must work out its own means of salvation.' Similarly, marxist critics of Republicanism should recall that it was Lenin himself, writing in defence of the 1916 Rising, who observed that 'Whoever expects a "pure" revolution will never live to see one.'

Of course, just as there have always been contradictions within Irish Republicanism, there are contradictions within the Provisional movement. For example, although the IRA Easter message called for mass participatory politics, the very secret, conspiratorial nature of the organisation would make it very difficult for members to be involved in such open, public agitation. But then, judging by the way British troops shot up unarmed demonstrators on Bloody Sunday, mass protest on the streets may not always be the most advisable tactic.

British propagandists see the Provisionals, or rather the popular feeling they represent, as a fundamental part of the 'Irish Problem'. On the other hand, without the Provisionals' military activities, just how many minds would ever have focused on the 'Problem' at all? The military tactics of the IRA have made sure that, rather than ending up in a closed file far from the public eye, Ireland is constantly forced under the nose of a reluctant world, which is exactly where it should be. Those tactics have also produced a response from the Provisionals' main opponents in Northern Ireland, the loyalists, whose politics will now be examined.

5.
The Loyalists

In August 1969, just after British troops had been sent on to the streets of Belfast and Derry, James Callaghan and Denis Healey told the Labour cabinet: 'The Protestants are in a majority and we cannot afford to alienate them.' This brings us to another problematic aspect of the Irish question.

The Protestant inhabitants of what is now Northern Ireland have always opposed the idea of an Ireland united and free from British presence. This is hardly surprising, since when the ancestors of today's Protestants first went to Ireland over three centuries ago, they did so with the intention of pacifying the most rebellious part of Britain's first colony. A contemporary chronicler observed of the Ulster Plantation: 'It will secure the peace of Ireland, assure it to the Crown for ever, and finally, make it a civil and rich, a mighty and a flourishing kingdom.'

The fairy tale has not exactly come true. The only phrase that still has some validity today is 'assure it to the Crown'. This was always the primary aim of the original architects of plantation, so in one respect at least they can be congratulated on the durability of their plans. So what is the secret of their success? Why do the Protestants of today maintain a 'loyalism' as faithful as it was in the seventeenth century? In the Irish quiz, these are the million-dollar questions.

Paisleyism

Socialism argues that in capitalist society the only progressive class is the proletariat, and that the proletariat must unite and organise separately around its class interests. In Northern Ireland, however, the proletariat is divided, has no political organisation of its own, and the largest section of it – the Protestants – appear to be the most reactionary social group in British or Irish society. Cynics who assert that socialism is fine in theory but impossible to achieve in practice would seem to have unanswerable proof in Northern Ireland, where the majority of the working class support, not socialism or even labourism, but the following:

> Both Romanism and Communism have absorbed the basic elements of pagan philosophy to bolster up their false and anti-God systems. Rome deployed and developed Pagan ritual within the framework of counterfeit Christianity. Communism, prior to the French revolution, adopted the pagan and pantheistic doctrine of creation. The resulting formula came to be known as dialectical materialism.

This very original definition of dialectical materialism appeared in *Protestant Telegraph*, the newspaper of the Reverend Ian Paisley, who in the 1970s became the leading political representative of the Protestant working class. In the 1979 European Parliament elections he received 170,688 first-preference votes, over 40,000 more than the combined vote of the two Unionist candidates who were his nearest opponents. In the general election that same year, his Democratic Unionist Party won majority support in the Protestant working-class communities, a trend which continued in the 1982 elections for the Northern Ireland Assembly. It might be wrong to deduce from these successes that the electorate wholeheartedly endorses the kind of philosophical illiteracy quoted above, but the general image Paisley projects – of a religious fanatic, a rabble-rouser given to interpreting events in terms of anti-Ulster conspiracies hatched by the devil, the Pope and the red peril – has certainly not hindered his political career in Northern Ireland. The incredible and uncomfortable truth about Paisley is that he is representative. Certainly he has influenced and developed the political attitudes of those who vote for him, but more importantly, he has survived in Northern Ireland longer than any other Unionist politician because he has never lost touch with his community. What he has always done best is articulate the fears and obsessions of the Protestant working class and lower middle class, and in doing this, he has come closer than anyone else to being the political personification of the Protestant masses.

Significantly, support for him is less evident higher up the sociological ladder. In previous years, the strength of the loyalist cause lay in the fact that it was an all-class alliance. For 50 years the Unionist Party (now the Official Unionists) dominated the governance of Northern Ireland to the extent that it was to all appearances a one-party state. Although their rule was accompanied by disastrous economic and social consequences, the Unionist alliance remained solid. There was the odd challenge here, the odd desertion there, yes, but the Unionist Party's hegemony over the Protestant population continued intact until the arrival on the scene of Ian Paisley. Although the party had been run by, and in the interests of, the Protestant middle and upper classes, the Protestant working class had always followed it like lemmings. This is so no longer, for what Paisley has done is split the Protestant community along lines which approximate to sociological class divisions. Unfortunately, while the Protestant workers have broken the chains that bound them to their upper-class leaders, they have broken to the right.

Ordinary workers?

To say that the Protestant working class has moved right requires qualification. Ian Paisley has distinguished himself from the leaders of the Unionist Party by taking up the sort of bread-and-butter issues which working-class representatives anywhere would concentrate on. He is a good constituency MP; he has advocated the nationalisation of Lough Neagh and its fishing grounds; he has joined hospital picket lines to protest against closures. It is also true that many of the leaders of the various paramilitary organisations which sprang up within the Protestant working class after 1968 had impeccable proletarian and trade union credentials. Billy Hull, who in 1971 led a strike at Harland and Wolff shipyard to demand internment, was a leading engineering union shop steward, and Andy Tyrie, who headed the Ulster Defence Association for most of the 1970s, was also a shop steward. Indeed, the growth of organisations like the UDA, composed of and run by working-class and lower-middle-class Protestants, seems to be a further indication that some form of class consciousness has arisen in the Protestant communities since 1968, even if a rudimentary one. The Protestant workers have even intervened in the Northern Ireland political crisis using that weapon of workers all over the world – industrial action. Witness the general strike they staged in 1974, which, although opposed by almost every Unionist politician of note, achieved its aims.

Yet to welcome these trends as progressive is to risk superficiality. People did not vote for Paisley just because he complained about the lack of inside-toilet facilities in their area. Just because Billy Hull and Andy Tyrie were once shop stewards does not mean that they are socialists. Just because the Protestant workers went on strike does not mean that they were developing class unity. Indeed, the aims of the 1974 strike suggest that the opposite is true, for they show the same exclusiveness which has traditionally characterised Northern Ireland's Protestants. One of the strike's aims – opposition to the proposed North/South Council of Ireland – insisted, in effect, that Protestant workers remain separate from other workers throughout Ireland. The other aim – resistance to power-sharing within the Northern Ireland legislature – demanded that all Catholics, working class or not, should be prevented from having any say in running the state. Far from being evidence of class consciousness, the 1974 strike showed that the Protestant working class was reaffirming its identity with Protestant privilege, and that the all-Protestant alliance was still a bigger draw than any notion of class unity.

Paisley's popularity can be explained in similar terms. His star first began to rise when he opposed meetings between the premiers of Northern and Southern Ireland, Terence

O'Neill and Sean Lemass, and rose higher when he fought the minor civil rights reforms of O'Neill and his successors, and then campaigned against power-sharing. Throughout, his rise to fame has been characterised by demands for tougher action against the rebellious Catholics. The 1979 election manifesto of the Democractic Unionist Party is typical of Paisley's priorities. It demanded that 'Ulster be put on a war footing', and called for 'full-time border security' and capital punishment for the 'heinous murders' committed by the IRA. The manifesto insisted that 'only a strong devolved parliament and government . . . with no room for power-sharing can meet the needs of Northern Ireland.' The only reference to social issues was a statement of opposition to the proposed liberalisation of the laws on gay rights and prostitution.

The hoary old themes were restated after the election. In July 1979 Paisley accused the Catholic priesthood of being 'deep in active service' with the IRA. Not to be outdone, Enoch Powell of the Official Unionists insisted in September that Catholic cardinals and even the Archbishop of Canterbury 'aided and encouraged' the IRA.

The point about these remarks, and the issues highlighted by the DUP in their election manifesto, is that they show a concentration not on jobs, housing, or any social or economic concerns, but on anti-Catholic bigotry, and the traditional Unionist relish for putting down the natives.

These obsessive priorities did not apply only to 1979. The decline of the Official Unionists is best explained by the concessions they were seen to have made to the Catholic minority, and by their inability to put down the rebellion. The Ulster Defence Association, the Ulster Volunteer Force and other similar organisations did not emerge because the Protestant working class saw a need to organise separately from the bourgeoisie, but because their activities – assassination campaigns against Catholics, for example – 'dealt with' the rebels in a way the Unionist government did not. The political struggles within the Protestant community since 1968 have been waged on the basis of who could sing the loudest version of the traditional Unionist refrain: 'Croppies lie down'.

It might be argued that all this was an organised conspiracy by middle-class Unionist politicians to hide the real bread-and-butter issues of working-class life from the masses. That the Protestant working class itself, through organisations like the UDA, insisted on maintaining traditional Unionism, suggests otherwise. The truth is that politicans everywhere emphasise what they believe will win them votes, and although Ian Paisley's bigotry is an expression of his own obsessions, it also reflects the obsessions of the audience to whom he is appealing. If this is true, it adds up to a rather unflattering picture of the Protestant working class. Let us probe deeper, then, for what lies behind this image.

The socialist explanation

So why does the Protestant working class behave as it does? The question has not received a great deal of attention from socialists, even those who have studied the Irish situation. Here is one analysis given at the Second Congress of the Communist International in 1920:

> Ulster, or more properly the North-east corner of Ireland, is the big manufacturing and industrial centre ... It is dominated by the only big capitalists in the country who are closely allied with the British bourgeoisie. Economically, the workers are organised in branches of the English trades unions, and politically the vast majority adheres to the Unionist Party, the party of extreme opposition to Sinn Fein and any form of Irish nationalism. One of its main factors, though steadily declining of late years, is its religious antagonism to the rest of the country. In many respects the problems of the Communists there are much easier, it being possible to rally the proletariat to their banner on the straight issue of the capitalist state versus the proletarian state. The lack of any nationalist republican feeling on the part of the majority of the

> proletariat renders them hostile to the establishment of an Irish bourgeois republic. With the exception of the anti-nationalist feeling, which is partly the outcome of religious bigotry, Ulster presents a problem similar to that presented by any large industrial centre, and for this reason may become one of the chief centres of the proletarian struggle against an Irish bourgeois state.

These views have not stood up to the test of time. Their importance is that they came up in the course of a discussion on nationalism, self-determination and socialism which was remarkable for its theoretical clarity. Yet as soon as the Protestant working class in North-east Ireland came on the agenda, perception ceased. One possible reason for this blind spot is that marxists and socialists had up till then paid scarce attention to the problem. In all their writings on Ireland, Marx and Engels had practically nothing to say on the Ulster question, while Lenin, although he compared the Ulster Unionists to the 'Black Hundred' gangs who were the bastions of landlord reaction in Russia, dismissed the Ulster Unionist rebellion of 1912–14 as no more than the excesses of 'a handful of hooligans'. Even in more recent times Irish socialists, with revolutionary optimism, have wished away the political affiliations of the Protestant working class. In 1969 Bernadette Devlin (McAliskey) made this prediction:

> I think that the Protestants may be the best of our supporters because they are the more radical people, and that their socialism is more radical as they have worked out their positions. The basis on which we can communicate with the Protestants is by being honestly socialist.

Some socialists, like James Connolly, who as a union organiser in Belfast had first-hand experience of Unionist workers, have been less starry-eyed:

> Let the truth be told, however ugly. Here the Orange working class are slaves in spirit because they have been reared up among a people whose conditions of servitude are more slavish than their own. In Catholic Ireland the working class are rebels in spirit and democratic in feeling because for hundreds of years

they have found no class as lowly paid or as harshly treated as themselves.

At one time in the industrial world of Great Britain and Ireland the skilled labourer looked down with contempt upon the unskilled and bitterly resented his attempt to get his children taught any of the skilled trades; the feeling of the Orangemen of Ireland towards the Catholics is but a glorified representation on a big stage of the same passions inspired by unworthy motives.

The labour aristocracy

The value of Connolly's assessment lies in the fact that it eschews vulgar socialist notions about all workers being the same, in favour of a sound materialist examination of reality. The reality is that as soon as the Protestant planters arrived in North-east Ireland they were given privileges. At first the privileges came in the form of land which had previously been occupied by the native Catholic population. With the growth of capitalism, the privileges changed in nature. For reasons partly accidental and partly the result of conscious policies adopted by the British administration, the greater capitalist development occurred in North-east Ireland. This meant that those who owned and controlled the major productive forces in Ireland were in the North-east and among the Protestant community. Restrictions on the political, social and economic rights of Catholics helped lay the ground for this development – for instance, not until the second quarter of the nineteenth century was a Catholic allowed to stand for election to the House of Commons. Within North-east Ireland a second layer of privilege was encouraged: one that discriminated in favour of the Protestant working class over its Catholic counterpart. Even when Catholics did find employment it was Protestants who were given the skilled and better-paid jobs. A wealth of statistics testifies to this development, which, as the next chapter will show, is still in evidence.

The Protestant working class, then, has had sound

material reasons for supporting the political and economic status quo. It may be fine socialist rhetoric to exhort 'Workers of Ireland unite, you have nothing to lose but your chains,' but the reality is that, in the short term at least, the Protestant workers do have more to lose than the Catholics. Compared to the material gulf between the Protestant ruling class and the Protestant workers, the distance between the Protestant and Catholic workers may not be great. Nevertheless, it is there, and the Protestant workers have shown time after time that they will do their utmost to protect the bird in the hand, rather than aim for the two in the bush – the Catholic and Protestant worker united in socialism. The support given by the Protestant working class to the 1912–14 Ulster rebellion is a case in point, for of course the establishment of an all-Ireland parliament in which Catholics would be in the majority would have meant the end of Protestant privilege. Similarly, although the 1974 power-sharing proposals were hardly far-reaching, they still contained a logic which the Protestant workers feared would ultimately threaten the superiority they had enjoyed in the Northern Ireland state. For 60 years that state had protected the 'poor white' Protestant privileges against the 'black' Catholics, an imbalance which the 1974 general strike and all of Paisley's campaigns aimed to preserve. To quote the threadbare Unionist cliché: 'This we will maintain.'

What would happen if factors outside the control of the Protestant population disrupted this status quo? If, for instance, the economic crisis of western capitalism plunged to such depths that the marginal privileges of Protestant over Catholic disappeared? Some socialists predict that such a slump may well come, and when it does, common suffering will drive the most deprived sections of the Protestant and Catholic communities together.

Such a scenario seems unlikely. In earlier periods of capitalist crisis – notably the 1930s – Protestant hostility towards the Catholics tended to increase. As jobs became scarcer, the competition became fiercer, and Protestant workers were more determined than ever to maintain their traditional rights to be first in the queue. Moreover, although the analysis so far has concentrated on the economic factor, the political consciousness of the Protestant community is shaped also by ideological, social and cultural forces which operate to reinforce the material considerations.

The Protestant culture

The importance of the religious factor is obvious. The badge of identification for the two mutually antagonistic communities is a religious one. Many leaders of the Protestant community, from Henry Cooke in the mid-nineteenth century to Ian Paisley, have been ministers of the cloth, and what is formally a religious organisation, the Orange Order, is allocated a statutory number of seats on the executive of the Official Unionist Party. Historically, it was the religion of those who took part in the Ulster Plantation which ensured their loyalty to the Protestant monarch in England, and this close connection of politics and religion still persists. A revealing and fascinating account of the way religious and political beliefs reinforce each other in the Protestant communities can be found in a series of articles in the *Irish Times* in April 1982. The writer was Roy Garland, a key witness in the Kincora controversy, which was a particularly sordid affair involving the homosexual rape of young boys at the Kincora Boys' Home. The importance of Kincora lay in the political cover-ups which were subsequently attempted. The man convicted of the offences at the home, William McGrath, had at one time or another been the political and religious associate of a whole series of Unionist politicians, including Ian Paisley and the Reverend Martin Smyth, head of the Orange Order and an Official Unionist MP at Westminster. McGrath was the leader of an extreme loyalist paramilitary group called Tara, and the shady deals surrounding the Kincora affair involved not only Unionist politicians but also British military intelligence, who exploited their knowledge of McGrath's homosexuality for their own ends. The full story of Kincora has yet to emerge, but what the Garland articles provide is an intriguing picture of the loyalist working-class underworld which McGrath inhabited, and which many Unionist politicians evidently felt constrained to pay some heed to. Garland began his story by describing his own environment, and went on to give an explanation of the views of McGrath and his Tara group:

> There were two strands of Protestant tradition on the Shankill Road where I was born. One was a colourful and exciting 'Kick the Pope' element which merged into a respectable Orangeism. The other was a fundamental Protestantism which regarded Orangeism as ungodly. One of William McGrath's objectives was to unite these two strands of Ulster Protestantism . . .
>
> His message was basically that the 'ancient' Protestant faith was dying out even in Ulster . . . In 1964 McGrath called a meeting. The objective was to discuss ways of bringing a 'Christian' influence to bear on the political situation . . . All present at the meeting except myself were British Israelites who believed that the people of the British Isles were descendants of the lost tribes of Israel. British people, therefore, had a special destiny to prepare for the return of Jesus Christ who would rule the world from Westminster . . . Ulstermen would have a special place in the events leading up to Christ's return and this was why Ulster had become a target for the enemies of God, Romanism and Communism . . . Throughout these years McGrath was able to bring his message to Unionist meetings, churches, missions halls and Orange Lodges. The message was always about the coming crisis and the bloody fight which was necessary to stem the tide of Romanism and Communism.

All this might appear ridiculous: the lunatic fringe of loyalism. But as Garland testifies, McGrath's group Tara had 'considerable influence'. McGrath himself had meetings with Paisley, Martin Smyth, and, in August 1969, even with James Chichester-Clark, the Northern Ireland prime minister. And McGrath was not the only influential loyalist who subscribed to such beliefs. The Reverend Roy Bradford, an Official Unionist MP assassinated by the IRA in 1982, was also a British Israelite, and the fundamentalist Protestantism of which this is one strand is widely followed in Northern Ireland. The success of Ian Paisley's Free Presbyterian Church is another example, as is the widespread influence of the Orange Order. While all these groups or institutions may attack each other for not being the 'true' Protestants, what they all share is a Calvinist fundamentalism which reserves for its adherents a personal dialogue with God. And a God, moreover, who has specially selected them to be 'saved' from hell and damnation, romanism and communism. Thus the Ulster Protestants, collectively, become God's chosen people.

There are other communities outside Northern Ireland in which this type of Protestantism holds sway – the southern states of the USA, for instance, or the white community in South Africa. There, as in Northern Ireland, there is political and sometimes physical conflict with the 'natives', even though in the case of the southern states the natives were imported slaves, and there, too, the 'chosen people' belief provides the moral justification for keeping the natives down. One can see similarities with the ideology of Victorian England which presented the great imperialist adventures in Africa, Asia and elsewhere as civilising missions in which, Bible in one hand and sword in the other, the white saviours would rescue the natives from ignorance and folly. If a few natives had to perish along the way, or if the missionaries had to take over the land, trade and government of the country in order to save it, so be it, for were they not superior people, mandated by God to do His work? Like 'natives' elsewhere, Irish people were depicted in Victorian cartoons with ape-like features, further down the evolutionary ladder than the English. In Northern Ireland, and more recently in Britain itself, the Irish natives as represented in jokes and song are stupid, dirty, and not fit to rule themselves.

Northern Ireland Protestant fundamentalism, then, is just one strand of the imperialist ideological baggage bequeathed to colonisers in many parts of the globe. It persists in Northern Ireland because the Irish majority are still denied majority rule over all their country, just as it persists in South Africa, for the same reasons.

But it would be wrong to suggest that the Northern Ireland conflict is essentially about theological differences. In fact the narrow morality of Northern Ireland's Protestants has more in common with Southern Irish Catholic morality than with English liberalism when it comes to issues like abortion and sexual permissiveness. What the 'chosen people' belief does is provide ideological justification for the economic and political privileges the Protestant settlers have traditionally enjoyed in Ireland. Even if those privileges were to disappear, so that the Protestant working class found itself in the same economic predicament as the Catholic working class, the likelihood is that the ideology would persist for a good many years. History books and political theory agree that ideology outlives the economic system which first gave rise to it. Britain today may be a third-rate and fast declining economic power, but the popularity of the Falklands/Malvinas War has shown how the jingoism which helped build the Empire can still be whipped up. It is socialism of the crudest brew to imagine that being reduced to the economic straits of the Catholics would force the Protestant workers to give their ingrained ideas a complete overhaul.

Loyal to what?

But perhaps there is another excuse for the behaviour of Northern Ireland's Protestants. Even if their loyalty to Britain does not always stem from the most selfless of motives, shouldn't their wish to stay part of the United Kingdom be treated with some sympathy? For, on the surface at least, Britain is a rather more progressive and equal society than the South of Ireland. The biggest flaw in this kind of argument is that the primary political principle of Ulster's Protestants has rarely been, and is not at present, fealty to Britain. For all their protestations of 'loyalism', the

'Unionists' have been quite willing to ditch Britain if and when it suited them. Reference has already been made to Edward Carson's threat to seek allies in Germany if Britain granted Home Rule to Ireland. This was no isolated incident. Similar warnings were given in the same period by other Unionist leaders. One of the organisers of the Ulster Volunteer Force, Major Crawford, said in 1914: 'If we were put out of the Union I would infinitely prefer to change my allegiance to the Emperor of Germany,' while another leading Unionist, James Gray, spoke of a 'spirit' spreading through Ulster which felt that 'Germany and the German Emperor would be preferable to the rule of John Redmond.' And although these statements warned primarily what would happen if a Home Rule Bill were passed, they implied that, link or no link with Britain, the Unionists would seek whatever means seemed necessary to achieve their ends. The ends in question, then, were not at all vows of obedience to the British polity. The period 1912–1914 was not the only time the Unionists' ambitions were shown to be less than 'loyalist'. When the 1945 Labour government came to power in the UK, the Unionist leaders were so fearful of its potential radicalism that the Northern Ireland cabinet discussed cutting the British link. Northern Ireland premier Basil Brooke told the Labour government that he 'might be pressed to put forward the demand that Northern Ireland be given dominion status, so that the Northern Ireland parliament might have full powers to do all that it thought necessary for the protection of the North.' What was in effect a demand for an independent state has been made often since then by loyalist leaders, among them Andy Tyrie, 'supreme commander' of the Ulster Defence Association, who advocated it in a *Guardian* article on 18 Febrary 1980.

Such recent Unionist questionings of the Union were a reaction to British government intervention since 1968. For, however scanty the civil rights reforms granted to Catholics, however oppressive British 'law and order', Britain did insist that there could be no return to the pre-1968 era when the Unionists ruled the six counties as they saw fit. The demand for independence seeks to revive those halcyon days when the Unionists were truly masters in their own house.

Scratch the red-white-and-blue surface of 'loyalism' and you find stark orange, for this loyalism is a loyalty to no one but themselves, the psychology of colonialists who take over a country and use all possible means to hold on to it. They care little for union with Britain, even less for union with the Irish majority, and the bulk of the Protestant working class care not at all for the unity of workers in general. They see enemies all around – the Catholic Church, communism, the South of Ireland, British governments who let them down – but they boast of no friends. The ideology they proclaim might have a glorious imperial past, but it has no future.

What will now be discussed is whether trade unionism – the traditional unifier of the working class – can offer one.

6.
The Unions

On 5 June 1981 Len Murray, general secretary of the TUC, said:
> Throughout the period of renewed sectarian violence since the late 1960s the general council [of the TUC] has followed the advice and example of the Northern Ireland Committee of the Irish Congress of Trade Unions . . .
>
> Make no mistake about it. The Northern Ireland Committee deserves and gets the unstinting support of the British trade union movement. Throughout all the years of death and destruction these courageous men and women have held the lines against sectarianism in the workplace. It is the only representative organisation in Northern Ireland which draws mass support from Catholic and from Protestant working people. It has maintained a link, a trade union link, across the sectarian divide. It has held working people together on the basis of policies for economic and social advance.

This is one of many tributes the Northern Ireland trade union movement has received since 1968. Michael Foot, at the 1979 Labour Party conference, complimented the unions on their 'strenuous and imaginative' efforts to deal with sectarianism. And in the words of the Northern Ireland Committee itself: 'The trade union movement remains as the one valid voice of working people. It is also one of the voices of sanity in the community.'

If these assessments are scrutinised, a contradiction

appears. The trade union movement is composed of individuals, acting collectively perhaps, but individuals all the same. So how is it that these individuals – approximately 300,000 of them in Northern Ireland – are exemplars of tolerance and non-sectarianism when playing their trade union role, while the community in which they live and work becomes ever more polarised? It is almost as if trade unionism is a magic potion which mysteriously transforms the Paisleyite or bomb-throwing Republican into a good honest worker dedicated to the fraternal solidarity of the common people. But magic potions are Gothic fiction. Is the self-congratulatory image propounded by Len Murray and the Irish union leaders as insubstantial?

To answer this it is necessary to look back at the tortured history which led to the establishment of the Northern Ireland Committee of the Irish Congress of Trade Unions.

The history

The Irish Trade Union Congress (ITUC) was formed in 1894. All the affiliated unions were British-based, and the founding of the ITUC did not imply a political separation between the two islands; like the Scottish and Welsh TUCs, it was part of a regional British structure. The formative years of the ITUC were characterised by a conscious avoidance of the controversy which divided Irish workers, although most of the leading ITUC members tended to sympathise with Home Rule.

The first decade of the twentieth century brought with it hard choices which trade unionists, like the rest of Irish society, could no longer avoid. One factor was the growth of a national and separatist sentiment in Ireland. A related issue was the establishment of Irish-based unions, starting with Jim Larkin's Irish Transport and General Workers' Union in 1909. Another factor was the rise of the Labour Party in Britain.

These combined to produce a heated debate within the ITUC about what form of political organisation it should support. The most famous example of this was a polemic between James Connolly and leading Belfast trade unionist William Walker, over whether unions in Ireland should affiliate to the British Labour Party or form their own Irish Labour Party in favour of Irish separatism. Connolly secured an important victory when the 1912 ITUC conference agreed to form a separate Labour Party.

This decision brought problems for union leaders in Ireland. The most industrialised area in the country was Belfast, where a large majority of union members were hostile to anything that smacked of an endorsement of Irish independence. By 1916, however, with Larkin in the USA and Connolly executed in the Easter Rising, much of the militancy of the ITUC had evaporated. Abstentionism on the unfolding Irish national revolution was one result. The official position of the ITUC executive on the Rising was that it 'is not our place to enter into a discussion as to the right or wrong, the wisdom or folly of the revolt.' When the 1918 general election turned out to be dominated by the issue of Irish independence, the Irish labour movement again stepped aside. At first, the Irish TUC and Labour Party – then a single organisation – decided to contest the election, promising that its successful candidates would boycott the Westminster parliament. This boycott was to be an expression of protest against British military policy in Ireland, rather than a refusal on principle to recognise Westminster's right to legislate for Ireland, as was the case with Sinn Fein's principled abstentionism.

This compromise satisfied nobody. Trade unionists in the North who supported the link with Britain were unhappy with the proposed boycott, while those in the South felt it was too partial a measure, compared to thoroughgoing abstentionism. The easiest way out was not to stand at all, which was what the Irish TUC and Labour Party finally chose to do.

For the development of socialist politics in Ireland, and certainly in the South, this abstentionism turned out to be a self-inflicted wound from which the Irish labour movement has not yet recovered. Henceforth the Irish Labour Party (which became organisationally separate from the ITUC in

1930) was to play no more than a minor role in Irish politics. The ITUC held together, at least for a while, but it was politically toothless.

After the establishment of the two Irish states in 1921 the Irish trade union movement tried to avoid the consequences of partition. This was problematic, since British and Irish-based unions were in competition for members throughout the 32 counties, and were using their respective nationalisms to attract recruits. The formal split came over the issue of neutrality in the Second World War. Ten Irish-based and strict neutralist unions left the ITUC to form the Congress of Irish Unions. Those who remained in the ITUC effectively endorsed partition by establishing a powerful Northern Ireland Committee. The cracks were papered over in 1959, with all the unions coming together to form the Irish Congress of Trade Unions, and although the Northern Ireland Committee remained as part of the new organisation, it became increasingly autonomous. Political divisions remained: in the South the Irish Labour Party was formally opposed to partition, whereas the Northern Ireland Labour Party had declared in favour of the British link in 1949. At times the same trade unions were affiliated to both organisations, although the Northern Ireland Labour Party never received substantial union support.

This illustrates a crucial difference between the labour movements in Britain and Ireland. Affiliations to the Labour Party allow British trade unions politically to unite the majority of the working class, at least on paper. In Ireland, even trade union unity can only be sustained if politics – or the main issue of partition – is avoided. Trade union leaders justify their avoidance of the constitutional question by saying that it is the only way to maintain unity on economic and social issues. The flaw in this argument is that in Northern Ireland there is no iron curtain between the concerns of everyday trade unionism and the wider political question of partition. One example of the overlap is the civil rights controversy of the late 1960s, and the shifting approach taken to it by the Northern Ireland Committee of the Irish Congress of Trade Unions.

The civil rights intervention

To its credit, the Northern Ireland Committee was one of the first organisations to highlight civil rights abuses. In 1966 an NIC delegation presented premier Terence O'Neill with the document *Citizens' Rights in Northern Ireland*, which included the demand for an ombudsman to look into complaints of religious discrimination. O'Neill took no action, and in the following year a number of leading trade unionists were among those who formed the Civil Rights Association. The CRA was a cautious organisation, although it was often unable to control those who rallied to its cause. When the street demonstrations began and drew physical reprisals from the police and the loyalists, the Northern Ireland Committee, although it never actually supported the civil rights marches, continued to press for reforms. In August 1969 the NIC produced *Programme for Peace and Progress*, which proposed UK control of security, an ombudsman, and a community relations board. There was also to be a legal ban on incitement to religious hatred, a public service commission to oversee public sector employment, and a central organisation for housing allocation. The demands were accompanied by an important political statement, which declared that the constitutional position of Northern Ireland 'cannot be changed except by the democratic decision of the majority of the people of Northern Ireland'.

This declaration resembled the position of many people in the civil rights movement – that the issue was civil rights, not partition. No doubt the NIC also felt that, as the rest of its statement endorsed the civil rights cause, a certain balance had to be restored by sanctioning the Unionist view on partition. However, the fact that the issue was raised in the programme at all represented a break with the past practices of the NIC, and undermined its professed position of having no view on the constitutional question.

The problems which the trade union leadership had to contend with were apparent in the workplaces, and never more so than in August 1969 in the Belfast shipyards of Harland and Wolff. Harland and Wolff had a history of sectarianism, with Catholics and, at times, socialists being driven out of the yard by loyalist mobs. With the new 'troubles' – anti-police riots in Derry, attacks on Catholic areas in Belfast, and the eventual arrival of the British troops – it was feared that once again the large Protestant majority in the shipyard would turn on their Catholic workmates. The trade union leadership made determined efforts to prevent this happening, and in this they were successful. Shop steward Sandy Scott received an MBE for his peacemaking, and the events at Harland and Wolff that August were subsequently enshrined in the annals of Irish labour as trade unionism's finest hour.

However, the reality was not so grand. The motion drawn up by the shop stewards and presented to the workers on 15 August declared:

> This mass meeting of shipyard workers calls on the people of Northern Ireland for the immediate restoration of peace throughout the community. We recognise that the continuation of the present civil disorder can only end in economic disaster. We appeal to all responsible people to join with us in giving a lead to break the cycle of mutual recrimination arising from day-to-day events . . . Furthermore, we demand that the government and the forces of law and order take stronger measures to maintain the peace.

No amendments or counter-motions were allowed. Those invited to speak from the platform included the Unionist Lord Mayor of Belfast, Unionist government minister Roy Bradford, and a Protestant clergyman. No one spoke against the motion, which was carried unanimously.

So what did this represent? Politically, the motion said very little: it was like agreeing to agree that sin was sinful. The one political demand it did contain – a call for stronger law and order – was a concession to Unionism. Public representatives of Unionism were used by the stewards to lend authority to the resolution, and no opposition was permitted.

It could be said that merely by calling the meeting the

shop stewards showed political and physical courage. Yet the way it was conducted was designed to stifle differences. No matter where they are voted on, motions that are carried unanimously are invariably rather meaningless, and rarely can any long-term significance be attached to them. So it was with the resolution adopted that day at Harland and Wolff. It did not prove that trade unionism could put out the fires of sectarianism, merely that trade unionism need not necessarily be engulfed by the flames.

The following years underlined how limited was the trade union movement's capacity to intervene in the growing political and, at times, sectarian conflict in which so many of its members were involved.

The challenge of sectarianism

At Harland and Wolff the loyalist ideology of the majority of the workforce soon reasserted itself. For instance, just before internment was introduced in August 1971, shop stewards added their weight to the demands for it by leading the rank and file in a token strike, while in the 1974 loyalist strike against power-sharing and a Council of Ireland (see Chapter 5), many of the leaders were Harland and Wolff shop stewards. The NIC and British TUC focused a combined attempt to break the 1974 strike on the Harland and Wolff yards, with a 'back to work' march led by Len Murray. But with fewer than 200 workers turning out, the march was a fiasco, and the shipyard stayed empty.

If the 1970s saw no recurrence of the previous anti-Catholic violence in the shipyard, it has to be said that, even from a loyalist point of view, there was little reason for aggression. This was because, during the 1970s, the number of Catholics working at the shipyard gradually decreased – from 2,000 in the late 1960s to approximately 400 in 1980 – a proportional as well as a quantitative decline. A confidential report of the government's Fair Employment Agency, leaked to the *Irish Times* in April 1982, disclosed that there was not one Catholic among the skilled fitters and similar trades employed at Harland and Wolff.

Discrimination was not confined to the shipyard. The same FEA report revealed that at Short's aircraft factory only 4 to 8 per cent of the skilled workers were Catholic. The percentage was similar in other companies, whether multinational subsidiaries – the US-controlled Hughes Tool Company for instance – or local firms, such as Hugh J. Scott Engineering, or even public-controlled bodies, like the Northern Ireland Electricity Service. In all these concerns Catholics were grossly under-represented, especially at the level of skilled trades and management. In 1978 an earlier FEA report had concluded that there were two-and-a-half times as many Catholics as Protestants unemployed in Northern Ireland, and that, of those in work, 'the model Protestant male is a skilled worker, whereas the model Roman Catholic is unskilled.' Yet another report issued by the FEA in 1980 indicated that the proportion of Catholics in lower-status jobs, as opposed to skilled trades, 'could increase in the next decade'.

What is illustrated here is the failure of those in Northern Ireland who promised voluntaristic or legislative solutions to discrimination, among them the optimists of the Northern Ireland Committee of the Irish Congress of Trade Unions. Yet on the surface the NIC was remarkably successful. Almost all the reforms suggested in the 1969 *Programme for Peace and Reconstruction* were implemented. Neither peace nor reconstruction ensued, however, for the reforms made little material difference to the Catholic working class. Within two or three years they grew weary of demanding civil rights, and began to focus their attention on the traditional enemies – partition and the presence of the British in Ireland. This in turn reinforced the conspiracy theories of Protestant leaders who had claimed all along that the civil rights campaign was just another Republican plot. The slide towards inter-community conflict, as well as the hostilities between the British Army and the working-class Catholic ghettos, was as inevitable as it was deadly.

Unwilling to admit that their efforts were incapable of bridging the political chasm between their members, the trade union leaders declined to acknowledge the reality around them. The NIC continued to pretend that sectarianism would be vanquished if only one or two more reforms were implemented. Central to its 1971 *Programme for Peace, Employment and Reconstruction* was a call for a Bill of Rights, which seemed rather like an instruction to the working class to be nice to each other. Naivety became an increasing feature of the NIC and ICTU statements on Northern Ireland. Pious hopes, rather than concrete policies, became the order of the day. The 1973 ICTU conference passed this resolution:

> Congress reiterates its support for all who seek an abolition of discrimination, the ending of violence and the adoption of positive policies to protect human rights, abolish poverty, introduce a more equitable social order and develop the resources of the region [Northern Ireland] in the interest of the people.

Those kind of 'wouldn't it be lovely' sentiments culminated in 1976 with the launching of the NIC Better Life for All Campaign, which called for 'the right to live free from threats of violence . . . the right to associate freely . . . the right to well-paid work . . . the right to free and full education . . . the right to adequate social services'. Who could disagree with such worthy aspirations? Indeed, no one did. *TU News*, a broadsheet launched by the NIC to promote the campaign, proudly reported in its second issue that representatives of the Labour, Liberal and Conservative parties had all officially endorsed the initiative. As in the case of the Harland and Wolff resolution, this unanimity was an indication of the emptiness of the campaign, rather than evidence of a strong consensus.

Occasionally, leading trade unionists admitted as much. At the 1973 ICTU conference J.McDonald of the Irish Transport and General Workers' Union commented on the resolution quoted above:

> The motion is non-contentious, it will be passed unanimously, probably to suitable applause, and then if past events are anything to go by, will be forgotten by the majority of the delegates . . . the trade union movement which is supposed to mirror the aspirations

and ideals of Irish workers, claps itself on the back, sits smugly amidst the carnage and human wreckage and receives well-publicised medals for peace-keeping . . .
Let us be honest with ourselves and our people. The trade union movement in Northern Ireland stands guilty of the charge of inactivity when working-class leadership was never more necessary.

The challenge unanswered

The accusation of inactivity may seem unfair in the light of the statements, plans and campaigns which bear the signature of the trade union leadership. But there is a difference between saying and doing. The 1982 annual report of the Fair Employment Agency echoed McDonald:

The Agency is not happy that all workers' organisations are making every effort to encourage the acceptance of genuine equality of opportunity. The trade unions have indicated their support for the work of the Agency and the permanent officials work hard to push the concept at a national level but they, too, would prefer to see the problem left for others to resolve. Just as an employer may be tempted to say, 'I would do more to push equality of opportunity if I were not as afraid of adverse reaction from the workforce,' so the trade unions will say, 'We could do more to push the understanding of equality of opportunity if only the employers would support us.' In such a situation it is easy to pass the buck . . . From the trade unions . . . we would call for pressure to be placed on managements who do not conform to an equal opportunity policy to develop their practice in line with the Agency's advice. To do this requires the co-operation of the rank-and-file membership but it is a commitment of the community as a whole to provide equal opportunity in employment.

This criticism makes one point which is crucial to an understanding of the limitations of trade unionism in Northern Ireland. Whatever the opinions of the union leadership, and however progressive their policies look on paper, to be effective, they must have the support of the rank and file – and the dominant majority of the rank and file are loyalist. Just under two-thirds of the Northern Ireland population are Protestant, but because of discrimination the percentage of those in employment and unions would be higher: 90 per cent of union members, for instance, prefer to be in British-based unions. It would be a slander to suggest that all these Protestant trade unionists are sectarians, but the election votes Ian Paisley received in the late 1970s and early 1980s showed that too many of them were – enough, certainly, to make any attempt to involve the rank and file in destroying sectarianism look like a utopian dream. Which meant, as a delegate to the 1974 ICTU conference noted:

> The policies of the ICTU and the Northern Ireland Committee in 1969, 1971 and 1973 stressed the principle of equality, social justice, employment, prosperity and peace. We have provided the guidelines for the unity and increased strength of the unions. Have we involved the rank and file in the formation of those policies? As it was, the documents were handed down to the membership.

What else could the ICTU and the Northern Ireland Committee do? Merely to keep their membership affiliated to an all-Ireland organisation was an achievement. As John Coulthard, a leading member of the NIC, said at the 1974 conference, 'If we were to take a postal ballot of paid-up members in Northern Ireland tomorrow, the British-based unions would disaffiliate [from the ICTU] and we have to accept this as a fact.'

All this suggests that even if the trade union leaders had had the political will actively to promote non-sectarianism among their membership, it would have run counter to their own material and bureaucratic interests: there would have been a rank-and-file revolt and the Irish trade union movement would have split. The lessons of 1944–58, when the movement had divided, were not forgotten. The contentious issues were avoided. Thus the NIC refused to condemn publicly and unequivocally repressive government measures such as internment, the Prevention of Terrorism Act, and the Emergency Powers Act. Such criticisms as were made expressed concern at the individual effects of repression, rather than condemning the repression itself. The following objection to the Prevention of Terrorism Act is fairly typical of the NIC approach:

> In one case a person who was arrested, detained and subsequently served with an exclusion notice has had to turn down offers of employment in Europe or the Middle East since the agents for the companies concerned operate from London and would require applicants to attend there for interview, from which they are debarred by the notice.

On other occasions the NIC travelled the same road as the wholehearted supporters of the 'law and order' lobby. Its attitude to the 1977 loyalist strike was a case in point.

Leaders and strikers

Led by Ian Paisley, the 1977 strike sought to return Northern Ireland to the days of unfettered loyalist rule, and demanded in the meantime firmer 'security' measures by Britain. Apart from Paisley's own Democratic Unionist Party, the strike was opposed by all the major political parties in Northern Ireland. The NIC also came out against it, but the manner of its opposition was instructive, for it concentrated its fire less on the politics of the strike than on the economic effects. In the run-up to the strike the NIC's first public statement began:

> It must be firmly stated that disruption on the lines indicated will create dangers for existing employment in many sectors of industry and will further threaten the creation of new employment opportunity and investment on which so much of the future of Northern Ireland depends.

This may have been true, but then so it would have been of any widespread strike action, no matter why it was called. In that respect it was an argument against strikes in general and not the May 1977 one in particular. The NIC statement did go on to mention the strike's aims, but in a tone far from hostile. Instead of arguing against the calls for greater 'security' – to Catholics, a euphemism for repression – the statement complained that the strike would impede the pursuit of all 'men of violence' – to Protestants, a synonym for Republicans. When the strike began this theme was reiterated by Harold Binks, chairperson of the NIC:

> It is evident that there is a widespread demand throughout Northern Ireland for better security and for better protection for life and property . . . all sections of the community have a valuable role to play in the fight against terrorism. They should formulate specific suggestions for improvements and should pass them on to government through legitimate channels.

Perhaps it was necessary for the NIC to make these concessions to the prejudices of the loyalist majority among their membership, to stop them backing the strike. If that was the case, it would be out of turn to blame the individual NIC leaders for failing to disassociate themselves from all the aims of the Paisleyites. It would also be inappropriate to try to unearth some kind of 'bureaucratic sell-out' of the rank and file, since probably the only 'sell-out' the NIC leaders were guilty of was a failure to reflect fully the extremely intransigent loyalism of most of their membership. If the NIC had tried to mount a frontal assault on the sectarianism in its rank and file, the trade union movement would have been destroyed.

This once again illustrates the limitations of trade unionism in Northern Ireland: its non-sectarianism is timid, its 'unity' impotent, its politics faint-hearted. And, in Northern Ireland, this sort of passivity is no answer at all.

There have been times, before and after partition, when economic struggles have led to a temporary unity between Catholic and Protestant workers. For example, there was the 1907 Belfast strike led by Jim Larkin, which united Protestants and Catholics in different trades, and the 1932 Belfast campaign against unemployment, in which they fought side by side against the Unionist government. Both these actions were short-lived, however. In 1907 the temporary unity was fractured by the re-emergence of the Home Rule controversy, and the Unionists' insistence that it was the main issue – which in fact it was. The unity of 1932 was destroyed when the Unionist government consciously and publicly promoted increased discrimination against Catholics as a solution to the problem of Protestant unemployment. On both occasions the Protestant dissidents returned to the loyalist fold.

This is hardly surprising, for a consciousness of wage struggles and the need for unity in them does not necessarily lead to political consciousness or unity. And, while there have been some – if very few – examples of unity on economic questions, there is no comparable example of political unity. Meanwhile, in Northern Ireland, the question of politics – particularly of partition – affects everything. It touches on who gets employed at Harland and Wolff, or who gets promoted in the Northen Ireland Electricity Service; it defines the narrow line the Northern Ireland Committee of the Irish Congress of Trade Unions must walk if it wishes to stay alive.

This is not to say that trade union struggles which are purely for economic reforms are unimportant. It is merely to suggest that their strategic value is overestimated. For example, in December 1980 the Fermanagh trades council paper *Workers' Voice* carried a front-page story headlined: 'Demand Better Treatment for Old Age Pensioners'. Now December 1980 saw the climax of the first hunger strike in the H Blocks of Long Kesh, yet not one mention of this was to be found in *Workers' Voice*. Instead, the key issue for them was pensions. Meanwhile, back in the real world . . .

7.
Why Britain?

On 20 December 1978 a *Daily Express* editorial described the membership of the IRA as 'not soldiers but sneak killers and physical cowards. Its leaders are not Nationalists but bog-fascists with personality problems.'

Apart from asking what a 'bog-fascist' is anyway, one might object that such a sweeping condemnation is a bit excessive. Not as far as the *Daily Star* of 30 August 1979 was concerned. For, after the IRA assassinated Lord Mountbatten the *Star* campaigned against everything Irish and positively begged its readers to do likewise:

> Every housewife who normally buys Kerrygold butter can switch to another brand. Every husband who enjoys a pint of Guinness or Harp lager can order a different brew at the local. Every family planning a holiday in the Emerald Isle can go to a British resort instead.

The trouble with this kind of propaganda is that it can turn out to be self-defeating. In the minds of the *Daily Express* and *Daily Star* readers, the gross image of the Irish presented to them leads to one simple conclusion: 'Bring the troops back home and let them tear themselves to pieces – that's all they deserve.' This kind of response was referred to in an *Express* editorial, also published just after the Mountbatten assassination, which reported 'scores of calls flooding into *Express* offices' – but, of course, this was hardly the response the *Express* wanted its anti-Irish inanities to evoke. So the paper hastened to remind its readers that bringing the troops home would result in civil war, and that 'Rivers of blood might be the Irish way, but we have long since given up that kind of gunboat philosophy.'

The public's opinion

The majority of the British public do not share the *Express*'s sense of national responsibility. Opinion polls during the 1970s and early 1980s showed that most of those questioned in Britain supported some form of withdrawal from Northern Ireland. In one survey published in the *Sunday Times* on 21 December 1981, 63 per cent said that if a referendum was held on whether Northern Ireland should remain part of the UK, they would vote against. In a *New Society* poll on 24 September 1981, 54 per cent supported the withdrawal of British troops, either immediately or within five years. In a MORI poll published in the *Daily Star* on 15 May 1981, the positive response to a similar question was 59 per cent.

At first glance, these figures might suggest a progressive outlook – that the British public side with the Irish against their own government, and believe that Britain has no right to be in any part of Ireland. But that would be wishful thinking. In the *New Society* poll only 21 per cent supported the idea of Irish reunification. In the MORI/*Daily Star* poll only 4 per cent expressed either 'a great deal' or 'a fair amount' of sympathy with the Republican hunger strikers in Long Kesh. These low figures show that the 'troops out' sentiment of the British public does not stem from a repugnance towards British injustice in Ireland, but from the opposite – a resentment at being unfairly burdened by the Irish, and a feeling that the best thing Britain can do is leave and let the mad Paddies fight it out.

Opinions such as these are moulded by British media reportage of Ireland, and find fertile soil in the national chauvinism which for generations has permeated all levels of British society. Yet there is a core of rationality also. For many people, there seems no obvious reason why Britain should want to stay in Ireland, so they conclude that it must be because of a sense of duty and a fear that departure would precipitate a blood bath. After all, sloganising about 'British imperialism' in Ireland is all very well, but the Belfast streets, far from being paved with gold, are a drain on the British Exchequer. One estimate published in the *Daily Express* on 29 August 1979 reckoned 'Northern Ireland is costing every man, woman and child in the United Kingdom about £21 a year.' The accuracy of this figure is open to question, but the fact remains that it would be hard to cook up an alternative figure which proved that British capitalism was profiting from Northern Ireland.

A consensus of opinion?

The *Express* and the *Star* do not speak for all of Fleet Street when they salute the presence of the Union Jack in Northern Ireland. In August 1978 a front-page *Daily Mirror* editorial called for the withdrawal of British troops within five years, a demand it has since repeated at regular intervals. On 16 August 1981 the *Sunday Times* proposed that 'Britain should declare its intention of renouncing its sovereignty over Northern Ireland.' The *Guardian* has also argued for alterations in the constitutional arrangement; for instance on 16 August 1979, when it called for a settlement 'putting England and Ulster farther apart'. And on 18 February 1980 the *Financial Times*, quoting Irish premier Charles Haughey's call for Britain to declare its interest in Irish unity, commented; 'Any British government that interpreted his words as unhelpful would be distinctly foolish.'

This pressure for Britain to find a way of extricating itself from its Irish mess has not been restricted to newspaper editorials. In May 1981 former Labour Party leader James Callaghan – normally the most cautious of souls – told the House of Commons that British policy had never worked, and never would work in Northern Ireland, and that departure was the only sensible option. Even the Thatcher government showed signs of casting around for an exit door. In December 1980 Margaret Thatcher and Charles Haughey had a summit meeting in Dublin, and the communiqué issued afterwards contained the following ambiguous passage:

> They considered that the best prospect of attaining these objectives was the further development of the unique relationship between the two countries.
>
> They accordingly decided to devote their next meeting in London during the coming year to special consideration of the totality of relations within these islands. For this purpose they have commissioned joint studies, including possible new institutional structures.

It was never explained in public what this really meant, but after talks between Thatcher and the new Irish premier Garret Fitzgerald in November 1981 another communiqué referred to the establishment of an Anglo-Irish council which was to include 'an Anglo-Irish body at parliamentary level comprising members to be drawn from the British and Irish parliaments, the European parliament, and any elected assembly that may be established for Northern Ireland.'

This plan was put into cold storage, so it would be wrong to imagine that great diplomatic changes were under way. But at the very least it did suggest that the British were dissatisfied with the existing constitutional arrangement between the two islands, the keystone of which is the position of Northern Ireland. Certainly, a number of Unionists and Tories detected a sell-out. In January 1981 right-wing Tory Nicholas Winterton alleged that the Foreign Office was 'determined to relinquish all responsibility' in Northern Ireland. The same claim had been made the previous September by Enoch Powell, the Official Unionist MP and former Tory minister, who maintained: 'The British Foreign Office is the inveterate enemy of Ulster as part of the United Kingdom.'

However fanciful these warnings were, what is interesting is the apathetic response they met with in the Conservative Party as a whole. An article by the London correspondent of the *Irish Times* on 28 November 1981 estimated that there were no more than 20 Tory MPs 'with even a passing interest' in Northern Ireland. Most of these, the article went on, were 'right-wingers who are essentially Unionists and seem to see Northern Ireland as practically the last remnant of the Empire.' The surprise is not that such a body of opinion exists, but that it should be so small. Indeed, the same article reported a senior Foreign Office civil servant describing these die-hard Tories as 'fascist loonies'. On 24 February 1981 James Downey, one of Ireland's most respected journalists, reported in the *Irish Times* that: 'Powerful members of the present Cabinet have let it be known that they view a united Ireland as the desirable, if not the only, ultimate solution.' Nor is this feeling restricted to the upper echelons of the Conservative Party. The *New Society* poll referred to earlier reported that, while 16 per cent of Labour voters favoured a united Ireland, the percentage of Tory voters was higher – 21 per cent. There was also more support for a united Ireland among members of the upper and middle classes than among working-class people polled.

An honest broker?

This evidence suggests a very different set of attitudes from those which held sway in the first 20 years of the century, when the 'fascist loonies' were well able to marshal the most powerful sections of British society to defeat the cause of Irish self-determination. There are several reasons for this change. One is the behaviour of the Northern Ireland 'loyalists'. The way they have conducted themselves since 1968 has evoked little sympathy. A community which elevates to the status of political leader a man seen by the outside world as a raving religious bigot is hardly likely to earn respect in Britain. And a 'loyalism' which, while pledging loyalty, seems to consist of thwarting reforms passed by British parliaments, is liable to become incomprehensible to those who are supposed to be the object of it.

The second, and perhaps the major reason for the lack of British support for the loyalist cause, is the feeling that there is nothing to be gained by holding on to Northern Ireland, no clear self-interest in retaining it. So how true is this suspicion? Why *is* Britain still in Northern Ireland?

If the 'imperialist booty' theory can be discounted as not fitting the current facts, so too can the proposal that Britain's present role is nothing more than that of an honest broker, keeping the peace between the two sides and favouring neither. The evidence of British partiality has been quoted in previous chapters, and can be summarised by noting that since British troops actively entered the Irish fray in August 1969 they have directed most of their activities against the Catholic community, and have consistently been used to back up the Unionists' wish to remain part of the UK. In the early 1970s, this was particularly evident in Bloody Sunday, internment, and the torture of Republican suspects by the security forces. And from 1976 to 1979, when, under the direction of Labour's Roy Mason, there was even more widespread torture of Republicans by the RUC, and the British Army was allowed to shoot on sight those suspected of IRA activity.

The loyalist paramilitaries never received this sort of attention. It may be argued that this was because they did not engage in violence to the same extent. Figures prove otherwise. From 1966 to 1973, for instance, of the 198 victims of assassination in Northern Ireland, less than one in five was killed by the IRA; when these assassinations reached their peak in 1972 and 1973 there were more than two Catholics killed for every Protestant. These statistics are recorded in Dillon and Lehane's *Political Murder in Northern Ireland*, a book which also documents a number of assassinations of Catholics by British Army personnel.

More generally, of the 2,092 who died from political violence in Northern Ireland from the start of the modern 'troubles' to the end of April 1981, 496 – just under a quarter – were killed by loyalist assassination gangs, and a further 208 – the majority innocent of any crime – were victims of the British security forces. If to these figures are added those who have been killed by loyalist bombs and other loyalist and security forces' violence, then just under half of those who died did so as a result of the activities of the loyalists and the security forces. These statistics are based on figures drawn up by the Northern Ireland priest Father Murray, a fierce critic of both the British Army and the Provisionals.

If British Army neutrality in Northern Ireland is a fiction, so too is its political equivalent. Every twist and turn of British government policy since 1968 has invariably been prefaced with the assurance that Northern Ireland will remain British as long as the majority of the population wish. Even the moderate nationalist pleas that Britain should publicly declare that it favours withdrawing from the North have gone unanswered. All of which would indicate a deference to the loyalist view that the Northern Ireland state is a legitimate political entity, and that its majority has the right to veto Irish majority rule.

But how does this square with the evidence that many in the British establishment would like to bale out of Ireland, and have little relish for the ideology of the loyalists? The answer is that while many would indeed favour withdrawal, they reject it because they fear the consequences. The Northern Ireland state will be respected, however unenthusiastically, until a more attractive option is presented, for although British interests may not be noticeably advanced by Britain remaining in Ireland, they could suffer a severe setback if it left. So what exactly are those interests, and what sort of setback does Britain fear?

Old generals

There is a jingle from the time of the Tudors which goes:
>   He that would England win,
>   Let him in Ireland first begin.

Contained therein is one of the major reasons for the Tudor reconquest of Ireland in the sixteenth century: Henry VIII feared that England's foreign rivals, especially Spain, would use Ireland with its Catholic allegiances as a base from which to challenge his rule. Similar tremors were afoot when the Act of Union between England and Ireland was passed in 1801, abolishing the devolved parliament in Dublin and placing Ireland under the direct control of Westminster. This legislation was enacted just a couple of years after the United Irishmen Rising had tried to establish an alliance between Republican Ireland and revolutionary France against the common British enemy.

Even when British politicians sought to repeal the Act of Union in the late nineteenth and early twentieth centuries, their proposals on Irish self-government invariably excluded the possibility of Ireland having its own armed forces or defence policy. In 1920 George Bernard Shaw, on behalf of the Labour Party, argued that although he supported Home Rule, 'It is impossible to treat Ireland as a separate country from Great Britain for military purposes. An invasion of Ireland would be an invasion of Britain.'

This concern did not disappear with the 1921 settlement. In 1949 the Labour government approved a secret report drawn up by civil servants, which insisted that 'as a matter of first-class strategic importance' Northern Ireland 'should continue to form part of His Majesty's Dominions.' Because of this, the report continued, 'it seems unlikely that Britain would ever be able to agree to Northern Ireland leaving His Majesty's jurisdiction . . . even if the people of Northern Ireland desired it.'

A British Commonwealth Relations Office document, which dates from 1951 but was only made public in 1982, sums up this concern with 'defence':

> Historically, Ireland, which has never been able to protect herself against invasion, has been, as she is today, a potential base for attack on the United Kingdom. It is the more important that a part of the island, and that one strategically well-placed, should . . . remain part of the United Kingdom and of the United Kingdom defence scheme . . .
>
> A United Ireland whose willingness and unqualified co-operation could not with certainty be relied on, which was neutral, or which was sharply divided internally over neutrality, would be a major problem in the defence of the United Kingdom and in the defence and support of Western Europe.

New generals

This kind of military/strategic thinking may seem out of touch with contemporary conditions. Not according to an article in the May 1982 issue of *International Relations*, however. This journal, incidentally, comes from the David Davies Institute of International Studies, an organisation of some influence among British policy-makers and which boasts former prime minister Lord Home on its committee and HRH the Duke of Edinburgh as its president. The article in question was written by Vice-Admiral Sir Ian McGough, former Royal Navy Commander for NATO's North Atlantic area. The following excerpt is worthy of note:

> The sea over the continental shelf, and the airspace above it, constitute the North Western approaches to NATO in Western Europe . . . To the north and west, Soviet forces would have to make the lengthy transit from the North Cape, and if their target was trans-Atlantic shipping, that transit would be increased by 500 miles or more if the shipping were to be brought in via the south of Ireland. Indeed the strategic importance of Ireland (the island) in any scheme of protecting shipping in the approaches to the British Isles can hardly be exaggerated. The current unrest in Northern Ireland . . . therefore, has serious implications for allied strength and unity.

The vice-admiral went on to argue that, for this reason, it was important for British governments to take a firm Unionist stand. In the course of his argument he offered the following audacious advice:

> As to the defence of the Republic of Ireland, which is the other state in the British Isles, very little needs to be said. The population is Celtic and Catholic almost to a man: and there is little doubt that any attempt to breach Eire's strict neutrality would be strongly resisted, although the total armed force numbers less than 15,000. The naval force consists of four corvettes: and in addition there are two fishery protection vessels

> ... It is fortunate for Eire that, placed as she is, and with a healthy economy, she need fear no invasion or risk of impoverishment. On the other hand, if Britain should once again find herself at war – and particularly with the Soviet Union – she could not accept a militant left-wing government in Eire, with the prospect of military facilities being not only denied to Britain, but made available to her enemy.

In a nutshell, the strategic importance of British control of Northern Ireland 'cannot be exaggerated'. Also, Britain must invade and occupy the Republic of Ireland, if the circumstances demand it. Henry VIII, it seems, is alive and well and dines out at Buckingham Palace.

Irish threats and promises

The timing of Vice-Admiral McGough's article was no accident. It appeared when the British government was widely believed to be considering options for lessening its control over Northern Ireland. The Anglo-Irish talks, which began in December 1980 with the Haughey/Thatcher meeting, had opened up this prospect and attracted attention to the issues later raised by McGough in his article. The Irish bourgoisie, cognisant of the traditional British concern with 'defence', offered reassurances. One of the most interesting appeared in the July 1981 issue of *Round Table*, a publication subtitled *The Commonwealth Journal of International Affairs*. The author of the article was Kenneth Whitaker, a powerful figure in the Irish establishment. A former governor of the Central Bank of Ireland and secretary of the Southern Irish Department of Finance, he had been widely accredited as the architect of Irish economy policy from the mid-1950s to late 1960s. Referring to the Anglo-Irish talks, Whitaker wrote:

> There has been speculation as to whether a defence pact might be one of the new 'institutional arrangements' to emerge from joint talks. Neutrality in an unqualified sense has never been a principle of the

foreign policy of the Republic. Its ideological
sympathies are with the West . . . No justification of
principle – other than unwillingness to aid the United
Kingdom to defend the border – was advanced to
explain non-participation in NATO . . . It has been
made clear that, as a member of the European
Economic Community, Ireland would participate in
any defence arrangements which the Community might
evolve.

Within this general framework, it would not be
unreasonable that more specific arrangements should
be offered between the two neighbour states in
recognition of their particularly close common interest
in security . . . Mr Haughey has said (Dail Eireann,
11 March 1981) that, when a satisfactory political
solution to the Northern Ireland situation is arrived at,
'we would, of course, have to review what would be
the most appropriate defence arrangements for the
island as a whole.'

Here, then, is one example – and there are many – of the bait being offered the British in return for their help in securing a united Ireland. And if the many leaks from both sides are to be believed, the Anglo-Irish talks did touch on this area. The possibility of a united Ireland joining NATO was the option most frequently raised. Both the Southern Irish and the British were thus acknowledging the supreme importance of Ireland in British defence thinking. The alternative to the Whitaker scheme, presented in the McGough article, arrived at a different conclusion, but the objective was the same: the priority of British security. For a while the Thatcher government seemed prepared at least to discuss the more radical Whitaker option, but then the Anglo-Irish talks came to a full stop with the Falklands/Malvinas War and the Irish refusal to give the British adventurers their wholehearted support. The subsequent freeze in Anglo-Irish relations was, at one level, a fit of typical Thatcher pique, but grave doubts had also been raised about the Whitaker option. For if the Southern Irish could not be trusted to support Britain in the Falklands/Malvinas what credence could be given to their promise of NATO comradeship in return for British withdrawal from the North?

The McGough option, meanwhile, had, and still has, one obvious drawback. Britain's support for the Unionist cause produces political instability, which in turn calls into question the long-term viability of Northern Ireland as a military outpost. With Britain's main opponents, the Provisionals, moving further and further left, with the 'loyalists' inclined to displays of most unloyal behaviour, with the situation spilling over into the South – for it can be argued that the Northern crisis has caused the fall of three Southern governments since the mid-1970s – and with the drain on British military resources, little wonder that Britain is willing to consider alternatives to direct control. On 28 July 1982, John Kelly, the Irish minister for industry and commerce, said in the *Irish Times*: 'I do not believe there are 20 genuine Unionists left in the neighbouring island [Britain], most of whose people would be heartily glad to be rid of the North, if they could get out without leaving a civil war behind them from which a second Cuba might emerge.'

The fear of an 'Irish Cuba' is another significant reason for the continued British presence. Just as Britain feared an alliance between Republican France and the United Irishmen in the 1790s, so today its ruling class is aware that a withdrawal from the North could destabilise all of Ireland and leave the country open to the radical heirs of the United Irishmen. (Anyone who thinks that 'Catholic' Ireland is an unlikely arena for radical revolution should remember that the most revolutionary populations of the 1980s have been in 'Catholic' Poland, 'Catholic' Nicaragua and 'Catholic' El Salvador.) The contradiction facing the ruling class is this: although Britain's presence in the North is designed to prevent an Irish Cuba, the longer that presence lasts, the more popular and radical their main opponents – the Provisionals – become. And the possibility of an Irish Cuba increases accordingly.

Such, then, is Britain's Irish problem. It is not one with which many Irish will sympathise, since it shows so clearly that it is self-interest which underlies British policy in

Ireland. As always, the security of the ruling class takes precedence. Which is why Ireland's problem is not Protestants or Catholics, the IRA or Ian Paisley, but Britain.

How, then, is this problem to be solved?

8.
Why Socialism?

The conclusion of this short study will try to answer various questions raised in the preceding chapters. For instance, why is Ireland an 'argument for socialism'? Is it possible specifically to indict the capitalist system for the modern tragedy of Northern Ireland? Why is socialism relevant to a resolution of the Irish conflict, and what form should that resolution take? Finally, why should socialists outside Ireland pay heed to events there, and what bearing have those events on their own political struggles?

The proposition that capitalism is responsible for the Irish situation requires qualification. English domination of Ireland predates capitalism, as does the major rationale for that domination – British strategic military/political interests. In this respect it may seem that Ireland's woes are attributable to nothing more than the geographical bad luck of being a small island situated in the shadow of a larger one. Pursuing this train of thought, one might argue that even if Britain became a socialist paradise overnight, it would, for reasons of self-protection, be obliged to keep a watchful gunsight on its Irish flank, just as the USSR has done with its smaller neighbours.

Tempting as these arguments are, the latter is just a little too cynical, and the former a little too simplistic. It is not land-forms which make history, but the people who inhabit them. It is the way in which the people of Britain and Ireland have organised their societies economically, politically and culturally since the late eighteenth century that has moulded the contemporary relationship between the two countries. There was nothing inevitable about the rise of Irish nationalism and its most radical wing, Republicanism. They arose as a reply to British exploitation, especially the economic exploitation carried out by the ruling capitalist class.

The oldest colony

Throughout the eighteenth century, when all European ruling classes regarded their colonies as economic investments, Ireland was one of the oldest. Three-quarters of the country was owned by British or Anglo-Irish families, most of whom lived in England and belonged to the upper strata of the ruling class there. At that time the value of Irish revenue to the English economy was roughly equivalent to the 1980 revenue from North Sea oil and gas. This helped finance an industrial revolution in Britain; while in Ireland a similar development was thwarted by lack of capital and by the discriminatory trade policies adopted by British parliaments to protect their commercial interests. Consequently, the Irish national movement attracted all classes: there was the native bourgeoisie, who saw their advancement being hindered by their English counterparts, and there were the lower classes, and, most notably, those victims of the land system – the peasantry.

During the nineteenth century the land question assumed prime importance, and it was the starving Irish peasantry who provided the muscle of the Home Rule movement in the 1870s and 1880s. Although land reform was forthcoming, and the bulk of the land was eventually transferred to the peasants who worked it, the bitterness produced by Britain's political and economic domination was by then too deep to be reformed away – especially when the political reforms of Irish Home Rule were repeatedly blocked. By 1918 the electoral success of Sinn Fein showed that the alienation of the Irish majority from all things English was complete. The savagery of the British government towards the leaders of the 1916 Easter Rising, and the ensuing repression, had been the last straw. In this catalogue of crimes one can trace the classic colonial/imperialist pattern – occupation, economic exploitation, denial of self-determination, and repression of the natives.

Another tactic of imperialism – divide and rule – was practised to perfection in North-east Ireland. Belfast developed into the most concentrated industrial area in Ireland, with the largest working class. From the end of the eighteenth century onwards, the division of that class into Catholic and Protestant, settler and native, was consciously promoted by British politicians, British generals, big employers, and the landed interests within the settler community. When leading Tory Lord Randolph Churchill commented in February 1886 that 'the Orange card would be the one to play', he spoke for many other members of the English ruling class, both ancient and modern. No sooner was there a prospect of working-class unity than British or Unionist politicians intervened to maintain the division. In 1912, Ramsey MacDonald of the British Labour Party observed: 'Whenever there is an attempt to root out sweating in Belfast the Orange big drum is beaten.' There are many examples of this. Take, for instance, the workers' unity which was shown in 1919 during a virtual general strike in Belfast. A year later, after inflammatory speeches by Unionist leaders, loyalists expelled Catholics and Protestant radicals from their Belfast workplaces, and the unity was effectively smashed.

The oldest settlers

Too often the Protestant workers were more than ready to comply in this division of the working class. On occasion they even took the initiative, against the wishes of the more middle-class Protestants. Discrimination in employment can be, and has been, overseen by the Protestant working class itself. The May 1981 bulletin of Northern Ireland's Fair Employment Agency contained evidence of this. The bulletin quoted from an 1865 report of the Belfast Riots Enquiry Commission, which discussed one field of public employment:

All this naturally tends to produce an impression amongst Roman Catholics, whether justly or not – certainly very naturally – that their chances of admission [to the workplace] would be small, and that promotion in it would be hopeless. The mode of filling vacancies also encourages this idea, and greatly tends to keep the composition Protestant . . . No proper advertisement is published inviting candidates to apply . . . The members [of the labour force] it may be presumed, circulate amongst their neighbours and friends, who are most likely to be their own creed, the intelligence thus withheld from the general public; so that without any direct exclusion of Roman Catholics as such, they are virtually shut out, almost as if there was a positive rule against their admission.

The Fair Employment Agency commented that this was still 'a very accurate description of the recruitment methods of many private-sector employers'. Without letting public and governmental organisations off the hook, it is nevertheless too simplistic to say that at every stage and level of the discriminatory process it is 'the bosses' or the Unionist politicians who actively exclude Catholics. In many instances the situation has become self-perpetuating, and the role of the contemporary employer or politician is as likely to be that of passive onlooker who permits the situations to continue, as it is to be that of active instigator.

Nevertheless, whether the division of the Irish working class is being promoted or merely sanctioned, that division is a legacy bequeathed by the particular development of capitalism in Ireland, and by the determination of those who reaped its benefits to maintain political control. With regard to Ireland generally, and the North-east in particular, it is easy to agree with that paragon of moderation, Shirley Williams, when she remarked at the 1974 Labour Party conference: 'We are paying the price for three centuries of past imperialism.' Although of course she could have added that the Irish have paid many times over.

So imperialism is the enemy, and because of this, the argument for Ireland is an argument against a specific economic system called capitalism, whose most developed stage is imperialism.

To come now to the second question – why is socialism relevant to a resolution of the Irish situation, and what form should that resolution take?

There are no surprise answers here. The arguments already advanced have been heavily in favour of British withdrawal from Ireland, and full self-determination for the Irish people. Two points in particular have been stressed. The first asserts the democratic justification for self-determination, in accordance with long-established socialist principles. The second flows from a historical analysis which pinpoints Britain's presence in Ireland as the major cause of past and present Irish 'troubles'. Neither of those arguments is original, or even controversial. Self-determination has, at least in theory, been a long-standing principle in most political circles, while the ill-effects of British policy in Ireland are accepted by most historians. When objections are raised to contemporary demands for British withdrawal they are more likely to be on grounds of practicality than principle.

The only significant exception is the theory which bestows on the Protestant community its own right to self-determination. The shallowness of the reasoning here is that the people who are to be self-determining are defined solely in terms of religion. For there is no other positive uniting factor within the Protestant community. The Northern Ireland statelet it occupies is not a geographical entity, but an entirely artificial creation. The majority in that area are politically, geographically and culturally detached from the larger United Kingdom they wish to cleave to. They do not comprise an economic unit, nor do they have history on their side, since never before in Ireland's history did the six countries have a separate existence from the rest of Ireland. Religion, it seems, is the only common denominator, and if membership of a particular sect of the Christian religion is deemed sufficient to define nationhood, then the entire map of Europe needs to be redrawn. The boundaries of Northern Ireland would undergo some interesting changes in the process. Catholic majorities in Fermanagh, South Tyrone,

South Armagh, North Derry and South Down would reduce the Protestant state of Ireland to even less tenable proportions than at present. And, to carry the logic to its conclusion, a new Catholic state of West Belfast would have to be created, in order to grant 100,000 Belfast Catholics their own right to self-determination. Which, of course, shows the notion of drawing borders according to church affiliations for what it is – an absurdity.

The blood-bath theory

Apart from religion, there is one other thing the majority of Northern Ireland's Protestants share: a desire to be excluded from a united Ireland. The wish of a minority to evade majority rule is not something which finds much sustenance in democratic principle. Especially when the motivation is a desire to maintain economic and social ascendancy over the majority of citizens. But the fervour with which this aspiration is expressed highlights the practical objections which are raised whenever British withdrawal and Irish unity come up for discussion. Chief among those is the 'blood-bath theory', which argues that the Protestants of Northern Ireland would fight to the last to resist Irish majority rule, and that if the British withdrew, the ensuing civil war would affect the whole of Ireland, and perhaps even Britain itself.

Only a very naive person would insist that as soon as Britain left Ireland blood would stop being spilled and perfect peace would reign. The blood-bath theory, like all predictions, can neither be conclusively proved, nor can it be disproved. On the other hand, the lessons of Irish history do allow a number of assumptions to be made. One is that political violence in Ireland seems inevitable until the Irish national question is buried too deep for resurrection. For the Irish majority, the injustice of partition and the British presence in the North-east is so self-evident that there will always be those who feel a moral and political right to challenge the status quo by any means necessary. Irish Republicanism is not sustained by Godfathers, priests, protection rackets or brainwashing, as the media would have us believe. Rather, it is alive today because of the obvious and colossal error of the 1921 partition settlement. In that sense the blood-bath argument works both ways. As long as the present constitutional arrangement between Britain and Ireland exists, there will be blood.

The question then becomes quantitative. Will more people die if Britain leaves or stays? Again, there is no sure answer, although the odds are that if Britain pulled out tomorrow, the violence would increase in the short term, and decrease in the long term. Of course, if Britain had withdrawn in 1801 instead of passing the Act of Union, the nineteenth-century Irish death toll from famine, repression and emigration would not have been so high. And if Britain had granted the Irish full self-determination in 1921, Irish bombs would not be exploding in Belfast and London today. And if Britain had chosen to alter the Irish constitutional situation in 1969, perhaps the body-count since then would not be over 2,000 . . .

There is something gruesome, to be sure, about these measuring exercises. They can also smack of political cowardice. For the assumption is that it would be the loyalists who would cause the blood bath if the British withdrew: it is the spectre of Protestant backlash which is conjured up. This is the argument of appeasement: even if the Irish majority wants Britain out, even if the British majority wants Britain out, nothing can change because a *minority* in Ireland threatens to resist with violence.

Just how much substance is there in this blackmail? There is no doubt that some sections of the Protestant community would react violently to a British withdrawal. It is also true that when the British government increased the strength and weaponry of the loyalist-dominated RUC and Ulster Defence Regiment in the 1970s they added to the threat of a Protestant backlash. At the same time, the Protestant community is not as it was before 1968. It is deeply divided. Once upon a time the Unionist Party enjoyed a monopoly on Protestant allegiance, whereas today there are three major parties – the Official Unionists, the Democratic Unionists, and Alliance – which have significant Protestant support, as well as numerous smaller political parties and organisations with roots in the community. The political solutions which find favour in the Protestant community are every bit as varied. While there is still little support for a united Ireland, options which have been put forward include a return to the pre-1968 devolved parliament, direct rule from Westminster, and independence. Martin Smyth, Unionist MP and head of the Orange Order, has even suggested that the Northern state should annex the three nearest Southern counties and restore the historic nine-county province of Ulster.

The traditional Unionist rallying cry has always been 'United we stand, divided we fall.' The fact that today's Unionists are tactically and organisationally disunited does not mean that they are incapable of launching an offensive against those they see as their enemies, but with the old singleness of purpose missing, any offensive is bound to be that much weaker. For example, if British withdrawal was total and immediate, what could the Protestants do? There would be sectarian attacks on Catholics, as there have been for generations, but to what end? Would the demand be that Britain come back? Would a call go out for an alliance with Germany, as happened earlier in the century? Would there be an attempt to set up an independent Ulster?

Only the last option would get past the starting-post, but even it would be unlikely to finish. The independent state which, in theory, could be established, in practice would lose approximately half its territory because of Catholic majorities, and would be impoverished and economically unviable. Those with most to lose – the Protestant upper and middle classes – would either leave the country or argue for trying to make do with a united Ireland. The ones most liable to do the fighting – the Protestant working class – would find themselves isolated from both Ireland and the British Isles.

This is all conjecture, but none the less it is extremely relevant. For there has been very little 'senseless' violence in Northern Ireland. The Republican violence has been part of a strategy to force Britain out. The violence of the loyalists has been focused on maintaining political control and economic privileges, and forcing the authorities to treat the natives' rebellion with utmost severity. There has rarely been an example of a 'motiveless murder.' That is why, when the blood-bath argument comes up, it is important to ask – what would be the *aim* of a Protestant backlash? The absence of a clear, rational answer undermines the prophecies of doom. Unless, of course, one assumes that the loyalists are simply mad sectarians, which would be merely to fall in with the traditional chauvinist and racist propaganda of the British ruling class: the natives, even the loyal ones, are not fit to rule themselves.

The cause of labour

What is certain is that British withdrawal and Irish unity would leave the Protestants, and especially the working class, bitter, isolated, even frightened. However, if the unification of Ireland produced little material change beyond the abolition of customs posts, green paint on pillar boxes and a wider circulation of Irish pound notes, there would be another section of the new Irish republic which would feel disgruntled – the Catholic working class of Northern Ireland. For they are the ones who have struggled hardest against the way their society has been organised. While their efforts may have been inspired by a traditional nationalist feeling, this feeling has been translated into action because they, most of all in Northern Ireland, have had the least to lose. If they had all been in secure, well-paid jobs and comfortable homes, they would never have rebelled. And because this present revolt has lasted as long as it has, they are all the less likely to be satisfied with an end product which feeds their Irish souls but not their stomachs. This realisation has driven the Catholic working class and its political representatives, the Provincial Republican movement, towards socialism, and it is this development which may provide the light at the end of the Irish tunnel.

For if a united Ireland fails to improve the economic lot of the Catholic working class, while leaving the Protestant working class angry and frustrated, then a whole range of new political possibilities and allegiances could emerge. It would be wrong, of course, to be over-optimistic. Class unity will not appear by magic, but will have to be worked for before, during and after British withdrawal. What can be said is that once the national question is solved the unity of the Irish working class will become feasible, because it is the national question which has divided it, and dominated its political consciousness for so long, to the exclusion of all other questions.

This, then, is how socialism is relevant to a resolution of the Irish question. Indeed, there is no other answer, and no other solution worth working for. The economic and social deprivation, and the sectarianism, can be overcome only when Britain leaves and the Irish working class fight not against each other, but for each other. Such a prospect may seem far off at times, but that does not make it any less worthy of struggle.

And then there is the final question – why should socialists outside Ireland concern themselves with and organise around the issue? This question is most relevant to British socialists, for it is their government's continued interference in Irish affairs which above all is responsible for Ireland's present state. Furthermore, if British withdrawal is to take place, the way in which it is managed, and the terms of it, could well depend on the stand taken by the British labour movement. If no stand is taken, then even if Britain did leave, its ruling class would contrive to do so in a way that would safeguard its own interests and frustrate the potential of a socialist Ireland. Such an outcome is far from impossible. Enough kites have been flown from British ruling-class circles in the last few years to suggest the kind of 'British solutions' that would be considered: a federal Ireland inside the Commonwealth, NATO and the EEC; dual British and Irish citizenship for those Irish people who wished it; a British/Irish council with powers to veto any change in the constitution or foreign policy of the federal Ireland; a joint British, Irish, perhaps even EEC 'security force' in the North; financial assistance to any former citizens of Northern Ireland wishing to settle in Britain.

This kind of 'British solution' would be designed to achieve a stable, capitalist Ireland committed to, and partially controlled by, British economic and military interests. It would bring little material benefit to the majority of the Irish, and would seek to block real Irish self-determination – that is, an Ireland owned by, and run in the interests of, the majority of its citizens.

Britain would find it difficult to impose such a settlement if its own labour movement had a solid policy which it was prepared to fight for. From a socialist standpoint, this policy would be relatively simple – British withdrawal, with no strings attached. That is, Britain would have no right to place conditions – whether military, economic or political – on withdrawal. The Irish majority, through some democratic form like a 32-county assembly, would decide on the nuts and bolts of withdrawal and what would follow it. Their decision-making powers would include the time scale of British military and political withdrawal – although it is likely that the quicker this took place, the less opportunity there would be for loyalist resistance. For example, if Britain declared its intention to leave within five years, the loyalists would undoubtedly conduct a campaign of violence designed to force the British to stay as custodians of Catholic safety.

Pending the achievement of a British withdrawal, socialists in Britain, while never losing sight of the overall 'Brits Out' thrust of their agitation, can take up issues which would strengthen this general strategy, and at the same time help to inform a reluctant British public about the true repressive nature of the British presence in Ireland. One such campaign could be to challenge the Unionists' right to veto constitutional change in Ireland, a 'right' which is based solely on the artificial Northern Ireland state, the fruits of a counter-revolutionary conspiracy to partition the country. Attention could also be focused on the denial of human rights contained in the Prevention of Terrorism Act and the Emergency Provisions Act.

This form of agitation would be different from the simple, single-issue 'Troops Out Now' demand of the 1970s. The value of this demand was that it highlighted the role of British troops in Ireland as being, not impartial and neutral, but malevolent. But, by the start of the 1980s, the counter-productiveness of the army in Northern Ireland had won greater acknowledgement. At the 1981 and 1983 Labour Party conferences, the majority of Constituency Labour Party delegates voted for British withdrawal resolutions, only to be out-numbered by the trade union block votes. Having achieved such victories among rank-and-file socialists, the 'Brits Out' slogan now requires greater elaboration. The issues raised by the simple shout of 'Troops Out' – specifically, the threat of a loyalist backlash – must be addressed. The changed realities of the 1980s must also be taken into account – for instance, by the end of the 1970s there were twice as many locally recruited 'security' personnel as there were members of the British Army operating in Northern Ireland. Advocating the disarming and disbandment of the British-born but loyalist-dominated UDR and RUC would both recognise this new balance in the security forces and point to a way of minimising the loyalist capacity for violence in the event of British withdrawal.

What is being put forward here, then, is a programme for British withdrawal, which could be based on:

- Britain to renounce all claims of sovereignty over Northern Ireland.
- The ending of the Unionist veto on Irish unity; support for Irish majority rule.
- The disbandment of the UDR and RUC.
- The repeal of the Emergency Provisions Act and the Prevention of Terrorism Act.
- The calling of a 32-county constituency assembly to set the terms and time scale for a full British military, economic and political withdrawal from Northern Ireland.

The cause of Ireland

Such an unconditional and complete British withdrawal would accelerate the development of a socialist Ireland because it would free the country from the straitjacket of British imperialism. For the British labour movement to support such a policy would be an act of genuine solidarity with the Irish working class.

The question of how it would advance the interests of the British labour movement remains to be tackled. A number of arguments can be listed here, similar to those put forward by the pioneers of British radicalism and socialism. A defeat for the British ruling class in Ireland – for that is what it would be – would weaken its position at home. Northern Ireland would no longer provide a training ground for 'security' methods which could eventually be used against the British working class. And the financial savings of a British withdrawal could build more than a few hospitals and schools in a Britain savaged by cutbacks.

There is another, less obvious reason, yet one which could have great significance for the progress of British socialism. Consider the other war Britain fought in the early 1980s. According to the propaganda, the Falklands/Malvinas War was waged to liberate 1,800 British citizens – although they had been denied British citizenship by the same Thatcher government a few months before the first shots were fired. Another version is that the war was just because the Tory government opposed a fascist junta – although that same junta had been and continued to be financed by the City of London. Whatever the immediate causes of the conflict, its spirit was encapsulated in what became its victory anthem: 'Rule Britannia, Britannia rule the waves'.

At the time, some socialists recognised the Falklands/Malvinas War as the burnt-out fag-end of the British Empire. The real shock was how few people in Britain, and especially in the labour movement, shared that view. The majority of the working class and its elected leaders cheered the Task Force on to teach the uppity 'Argies' a lesson every bit as vehemently as their ancestors might have cheered Queen Victoria's forces off on similar adventures. The immediate consequence was the devastating rise of Margaret Thatcher and her Conservative Party in the opinion polls.

It is probably correct to suppose that if the leaders of the Labour Party had opposed the Falklands/Malvinas War their popular support would have dwindled even further, for what was displayed so clearly in that period was just how deep are the roots of national chauvinism in the British working class. The strength of this prejudice makes socialism hard to imagine in Britain. It has been used against blacks in Britain, and against the Irish; it has been used to accuse trade unionists of 'holding the nation to ransom', and it will be used again and again.

This nationalism has nothing in common with the Irish variety, the nationalism of the oppressed. It leads not to radicalisation, but to support for the status quo, and is the enemy of progress and socialism. For that reason its opposite, internationalism, cannot be an occasional luxury, or merely a moral exhortation to workers of all lands to be fraternal. Rather, it is a necessity; without it, there will always be the temptation to put 'nation' before class.

For British socialists the fight for internationalism begins with Ireland, just as it did in the days of Marx, the Chartists, and the Levellers. 'The cause of labour is the cause of Ireland,' wrote James Connolly just before the 1916 Easter Rising, 'The cause of Ireland is the cause of labour.' There were few socialists who agreed with Connolly at the time, and as he sat in his death cell he predicted that English socialists would 'never understand why I am here'. Gaining such an understanding could help to liberate, not only the Irish, but also the British working class.

A Guide to Reading

Place of publication London unless otherwise stated.

The history of Ireland and the present conflict have attracted many writers. In this situation it is best to be as selective as possible. This guide therefore lists only those studies the present author considers essential for an appreciation of the historical and political background to the contemporary crisis.

The standard history of modern Ireland is F.S.L.Lyons, *Ireland Since the Famine*, Fontana 1973; the standard and marxist history of Northern Ireland is Michael Farrell, *Northern Ireland: The Orange State*, Pluto 1976. A further useful introduction is Liam de Paor, *Divided Ulster*, Penguin 1973.

An alternative 'Two Nations' view of Northern Ireland history is Paul Bew, Peter Gibbon and Henry Patterson, *The State in Northern Ireland*, Manchester: Manchester University Press 1979, and Patterson's *Class Conflict and Sectarianism*, Belfast: Blackstaff 1980. Other versions of the 'Two Nations' theory are contained in Tom Nairn, *The Break-up of Britain*, New Left Books 1977, and the British and Irish Communist Organisation, *The Economics of Partition*, Belfast: BICO 1972. A more detailed investigation into the partition settlement is Denis Gwynn, *The History of Partition*, Dublin: Browne & Nolan 1950, together with Lord Longford, *Peace By Ordeal,* Mentor 1967, a study of the negotiations surrounding the Anglo-Irish Treaty, first published in 1935.

The Ulster rebellion of 1912–14 is covered in A.T.Q. Stewart, *The Ulster Crisis*, Faber 1969, although perhaps the best, and certainly the most beautifully written account of Ireland from 1912 to 1921 is George Dangerfield, *The Damnable Question*, Quartet 1979. The Easter Rising is described in Max Caulfield, *The Easter Rebellion*, Four Square 1966, and there is useful background material in F.X.Martin (ed.), *Leaders and Men of the Easter Rising*, Dublin: 1966 and Leon O'Broin, *Dublin Castle and the 1916 Rising*, Dublin: Helicon 1966. For a participant's account there is Sean MacEntee, *Episode at Easter*, Dublin: Gill 1966.

James Connolly's participation in the Easter Rising has always been a matter for controversy among socialists. For this, and for many other reasons it is best to read Connolly himself. P.Beresford Ellis (ed.), *James Connolly, Selected Writings*, Penguin 1973, is a good introduction, while Connolly's main theoretical work is *Labour in Irish History*, Dublin: New Books 1967. The debate between Connolly and William Walker has been reprinted by the Cork Workers' Club, *The Connolly–Walker Controversy*, Cork: Cork Workers' Club 1974. The best biographies of Connolly are Samuel Levenson, *James Connolly*, Martin, Brian & O'Keefe 1973, and Desmond Greaves, *The Life and Times of James Connolly*, Lawrence & Wishart 1961. Emmet Larkin, *James Larkin*, Mentor 1968, is a biography of Connolly's comrade.

The history of the broader Irish labour movement is found in J.D.Clarkson, *Labour and Nationalism in Ireland*, New York: AMS Reprint 1970, and P. Beresford Ellis, *A History of the Irish Working Class*, Gollancz 1972. The Belfast Workers' Research Unit, *Bulletin No.7*, Belfast: 1979, includes an excellent summary of how trade unionism in Ireland has been handicapped by partition. Geoffrey Bell records the history of the British Labour Party and Ireland in *Troublesome Business*, Pluto 1982, while a summary of British public opinion on Ireland 1912–18 is D.G.Boyce, *Englishmen and Irish Troubles*, Jonathan Cape 1972.

The history of the Irish nationalist/Republican movement is well served by two recent studies, Sean Cronin, *Irish Nationalism*, Pluto 1983, and Kevin Kelley, *The Longest War*, Zed 1983. Also noteworthy is Tim Pat Coogan, *The IRA*, Fontana 1971 and J. Bowyer Bell, *The Secret Army: A History of the IRA*, Sphere 1972. For an examination of the loyalist community there is Geoffrey Bell, *The Protestants of Ulster*, Pluto 1976.

There are many published opinions of the present struggle in Northern Ireland. Eamonn McCann, *War and an Irish Town*, Pluto 1980, is one of the best, being an account of the opening years of the contemporary period by one of its leading protagonists. The same period is covered in the *Sunday Times* Insight Team, *Ulster*, Penguin 1972. For a British politician's view there is James Callaghan, *A House Divided*, Collins 1973. Robert Fisk, *The Point of No Return*, André Deutsch 1975, is a fine account of the 1974 loyalist strike, while Tim Pat Coogan, *On The Blanket*, Dublin: Ward River 1980, tells the story of the H Blocks of Long Kesh. Peter Taylor, *Beating the Terrorists?*, Penguin 1980, is a television reporter's exposure of the 'ill-treatment' of Republican suspects in the late 1970s, and M.Dillon and D.Lahanem, *Political Murder in Northern Ireland*, Penguin 1973, records the campaign of sectarian assassination in the early 1970s. David Bolton, *The UVF*, Dublin: Torc 1973, is one of the few books on contemporary loyalist paramilitaries.

The impact on Britain of the 'security' methods used by the British in Ireland is discussed in P.Hain, D.Humphrey and B.Rose-Smith, *Policing the Police*, vol.1, Calder 1979 and in C.Ackroyd and others, *The Technology of Political Control*, Pluto 1980.

An indication of the arguments that have taken place on the left on Ireland is provided in Austen Morgan and Bob Purdie (eds), *Ireland Divided Nation, Divided Class*, Ink Links 1980, with the two most informative essays in this rather uneven collection being ones by Michael Farrell, on the Ulster Special Constabulary, and Margaret Ward on women in the Republican movement. (These two contributors have subsequently extended their research and published full-length books on the subjects – *Arming the Protestants* and *Women and Irish Nationalism* respectively (Pluto 1983, both titles).) Other examples of discussions on the left are provided in *Marxism Today*, January 1982, in an article by Henry Patterson, and April 1982, in a reply by Geoffrey Bell. See Richard Chessum in *Ireland Socialist Review*, no.7, spring 1980, for a general critique of the Patterson/Bew/Gibbons school. The traditional marxist view on Ireland is also present in Marx and Engels, *Ireland and the Irish Question*, Moscow: Progress 1971, and *Lenin on Ireland*, Dublin: New Books 1971.